Only the Lonely

Only the Lonely

*Finding Romance in the Personal
Columns of Canada's Western Home Monthly
1905–1924*

Dan Azoulay

FIFTH
HOUSE
PUBLISHERS

Front cover photograph "Hornets nest" tent, Saskatoon, SK, 1907.
Courtesy the Local History Room, Saskatoon Public Library.

Cover and interior design by The Studio Group.

The publisher gratefully acknowledges the support of The Canada Council for the Arts and the Department of Canadian Heritage.

We acknowledge the financial support of the Government of Canada through the Book Publishing Industry Development Program for our publishing activities.
We acknowledge the financial assistance of Trent University, ON, for photographs.

Printed in Canada.
00 01 02 03 04/ 5 4 3 2 1

Canadian Cataloguing in Publication Data

Azoulay, Dan, 1960-
    Only the lonely

    Includes bibliographical references.
    ISBN 1-894004-55-8

    1. Canada, Western--Social life and customs. 2. Frontier and
pioneer life--Canada, Western. 3. Western home monthly. 4.
Personals--Canada, Western--History. I. Title. II. Title: Western
home monthly.
FC3218.A96 2000   971.2'02   C00-910955-2
F1060.9.A96 2000

Fifth House Ltd.
A Fitzhenry & Whiteside Company
1511-1800 4 Street SW
Calgary, Alberta, Canada
T2S 2S5

Contents

To Alyssa and Adam

Introduction

The *Western Home Monthly (WHM)*, published out of Winnipeg, was one of western Canada's most popular monthly magazines in the early 1900s[1]. It was eagerly anticipated by the region's earliest settlers, many of whom lived and toiled in almost total isolation, as it provided one of the few contacts with the outside world prior to the arrival of regular passenger-train service, automobiles, and radios. To the rural families and young homesteaders it catered to, the magazine also provided a wealth of useful and entertaining information on everything from farming and gardening to cooking, needlework, household decor, personal grooming, and etiquette. It also offered sketches of successful farmers, business people, politicians, and fast-growing towns in the region, sermon-like short stories and poems, editorials and articles addressing the burning issues of the day, and snippets of news about key developments in the rest of Canada and abroad. But for many years the magazine's most popular feature, without question, was its Correspondence column, which ran continuously from November 1905 to October 1924. Through this column lonely, isolated readers across the West, and indeed across all of Canada, could become acquainted with one another and exchange views on a variety of subjects.[2] The column became a sort of "correspondence circle," not unlike those in other periodicals and newspapers of the day.

What made the *WHM* unique, and what makes it valuable to observers of Canada's social and cultural history today, was the attention that its correspondents paid to matters of romance. Most of the letters, especially for the first half-dozen years or so, dealt almost exclusively with such things as courtship, matrimony, physical intimacy, and in particular, the qualities men and women sought in potential marriage partners. It would be fair to describe the column, in its early years, as a "matrimonial column." Both the readers and the editor certainly considered it so. Three months after the column was established, its editor noted that "correspondence on the Matrimonial question is growing.... We are requested by many young women and young bachelor readers to assist them in getting acquainted with each other with a view to matrimony. Whilst we are not conducting a matrimonial agency, we are most willing to assist in a proper manner to bring those who are matrimonially inclined together." As long as the writer sent along a blank stamped envelope, the *WHM* would forward letters for those wishing to become acquainted with other writers, as only pen-names and incomplete addresses accompanied published letters. By the spring of 1908, the magazine was exchanging about fifteen hundred letters each month. Three years later it was forced to restrict this service to subscribers only,[3] such was the volume of letters it received.

Not all exchanges were romantically inclined. Many writers simply sought correspondents for "fun"—or so they said—or wrote to pass the long winter nights on the prairie. But many, if not most, *were* soliciting partners, and therefore tended to specify the qualities they found desirable in the opposite sex. Many also offered their views on matters of romance, including courtship, marriage, and physical intimacy. By the time World War One began, Correspondence was no longer a predominantly matrimonial column, in the matchmaking sense—the virtual disappearance of personal physical descriptions being one indication of this.[4] But it continued as a forum for readers to air their views on romantic issues. The column constitutes a rich source of information on a topic that has been rather inaccessible and insufficiently explored—that is, what average Canadians in the late Victorian and early Edwardian eras looked for in a prospective spouse and what they thought about various aspects of romantic relationships.

All of the letters in this book are taken from the magazine's Correspondence column and represent, I believe, a sizeable and, geographically

Interior of a typical bachelor farmer's shack, c. 1910. The owner likely spent many winter nights by the lamp's light, reading the Correspondence column or composing letters of his own. Glenbow Archives/NA-2487-2

speaking, fairly diverse group of people. During the column's nineteen-year existence, the magazine published about thirty-three hundred letters, two-thirds of them before 1912.[5] These came from all regions of Canada and occasionally from Canadians living abroad. But the majority originated in the provinces of Alberta, Saskatchewan, and Manitoba, and many of the writers tended to be either independent farmers or ranchers or the sons and daughters of same.[6] Most of the writers were unmarried. Commonly referred to as "bachelors"[7] and "maids," they ranged in age from sixteen to sixty. The average age of male correspondents—who often wanted to establish themselves financially before marrying—was twenty-five. For female correspondents—who had been taught to seek a husband who could support them—it was twenty-one.[8]

The Canadian West was still very much a frontier area in the early 1900s. Populated by slightly more than four hundred thousand people in 1901 (excluding British Columbia), it was seen to hold great promise for young, enterprising individuals. The federal government offered 160 acres of free land to any adult male (single and married women were not permitted to become homesteaders) who, after three years, had established a home and cultivated at least fifteen acres. The relatively generous terms, coupled with the continuous expansion of railroads and the promise of unlimited prosperity in the "Last Best West," drew thousands of young people. Of the more than six hundred thousand immigrants who moved to the West between 1896 and 1914, most were British or American, with another 250,000 pouring in from central and eastern Canada, making the region predominantly white, English-speaking, and Protestant.[9] The West drew people from many other ethnic groups, of course, but their voices were not heard in the unilingual pages of the *Western Home Monthly*. Nor, judging from the derogatory terms used by some of the magazine's correspondents, would they have been particularly welcome. Apart from this, there is enough diversity of opinion in the letters to suggest that the editor was not unduly selective when it came to deciding which letters should be published.

Deciding which letters to include in this book was a difficult task. It is always tempting to select the most colourful or controversial pieces or to unconsciously (or not) skew the balance of the letters in favour of one's own views. But I have made every effort to avoid these pitfalls and to replicate the mix in the column itself. The letters are arranged in six chapters, each focusing on a particular aspect of romance, and in most cases only excerpts are included, to reinforce this thematic organization. Within each chapter letters are further arranged by date. This not only allows the reader to follow the lively and sometimes bitter exchanges between particular correspondents but to see how views and preferences changed over time in response to changing circumstances. One of the primary motivations of my research was to see how people's conceptions of such things as marriage and the "ideal" partner changed over time, and to determine why. What effect, if any, did the dramatic developments of this transitional period—rapid economic growth and urbanization, the emergence of movements favouring women's rights and social reform, World War One, and the

Getting a haircut—frontier style. Perhaps this rancher from Nanton, Alberta, is being groomed for a night on the town. Glenbow Archives/NA-2467-31

"roaring" twenties—have on Canadians' views of heterosexual relationships? Consider, for example, the following 1916 letter from "A City Girl" in Winnipeg, who criticizes the very notion of romance during a time of national crisis, in this case World War One:

> At a time like this when the very existence of the Empire is threatened, it is remarkable to note the general sense of

empty-headedness which appears to prevail amongst a large number of the readers who contribute to your columns. In the December issue, for instance, we have a man worrying because he escorted a young lady home in a thunderstorm, and she did not thank him. I very much doubt whether this particular piece of information is of any particular interest to anybody except himself. Surely, in times like these, the other readers of your magazine should not be forced to read such piffle. Are not the girls on Western Canadian farms interested in War Relief and Red Cross work as are their sisters in the towns and cities? Surely it would be more fitting for your correspondents to take a more serious tone, and write and tell us just exactly what they are doing for their country, instead of babbling about dark eyebrows and fluffy hair. The average individual is too serious minded now-a-days to be irritated by reading ridiculous sentiments, and it does not seem fair that a few shallow-minded boys and girls should be allowed to thrust their views on unimportant matters upon the rest of the *Western Home Monthly* readers.[10]

Some readers of the *WHM* agreed with A City Girl's condemnation, but many more did not, arguing that even in times of war—indeed, *especially* in such times—young men and women needed to distract themselves with romantic "piffle."[11] What is interesting are the changes that larger events brought about in attitudes toward romance. Readers will detect such changes for themselves, but I have made some attempt in the short introductions to each section to suggest patterns and present plausible explanations.

Finally, it should be noted that the letters have been carefully edited to best convey their intended meaning and original flavour. I have corrected errors in punctuation and spelling, but not in grammar, syntax, and vocabulary. I have made every effort, as well, to identify the geographic origin of the letters and, where unclear, the gender of the writers.

1   Only the Lonely

I want to have someone to love and caress
Someone to look at and call her my own,
Someone to cheer me when I am distressed
Life is so weary when I live all alone.
      Bunker Hill Farmer, 1907[1]

One of the most noticeable features of the Correspondence column is the large number of letters from people claiming to be lonely and in need of companionship from the opposite sex. Loneliness was not unusual in rural areas in the days before cars, radios, telephones, and regular mail service became commonplace, but it was especially acute in the early 1900s because of the circumstances facing the West's earliest settlers. Young bachelor farmers spent most of the daylight hours alone, working their land, caring for livestock, building and improving their homes, and fixing farm implements. They had precious little time or energy left at the end of the day or week to socialize with members of the opposite sex. Even if one were lucky enough to own a motorized vehicle or live near a train station, the long distances from neighbours and towns further inhibited contact.[2] The winter months seem to have been particularly difficult for male homesteaders, given the shortage of work to do on the farm and the long winter evenings cooped up in their modest surroundings. Young men working in the bush, or in lumber camps and railroad camps, were even more isolated.

There was also a large disparity between the number of men and women in the West during these years. In some districts, men outnumbered women ten to one.[3] In their letters to the *WHM*, men were forever complaining about the shortage of "marriageable women" in their area, a reality that stemmed from restrictions on the right of women to own their own homesteads,[4] greater job opportunities and recreational outlets for women in the cities, and the West's reputation—among eastern women at least—for drinking and lawlessness.

Two young bachelors from Grassy Lake, Alberta, c. 1906, find a few moments of respite during their long and usually lonely workday on the frontier. Medicine Hat Archives/PC419.1

When one thinks of all the hardships western homesteaders endured, it is interesting to note the hundreds of letters that cite, as one man from Alberta did, the "absence of the fair sex" as "the greatest drawback."[5]

Women were lonely too, because although they were in great demand, the men were usually too busy trying to "prove up"—that is, gain title to their land within the three-year deadline—to pay much attention to matters of romance. And women often worked in solitary circumstances themselves, as teachers and domestics especially. "The first thing that strikes one from the [United] States like myself," wrote a "marriageable widow" from Elkwater, Alberta, is the awful loneliness, for the men are always at work and the women forever alone (I am anyway).... I am house-keeper here and forever alone, rising at 4:30 A.M. going to bed at 9 P.M."[6] The letters from "Lonely Elnor" and "City Girl," below, suggest that even women who worked in the city were not immune to loneliness. What's more, women were historically more restricted in their movements than men. They were not permitted, either by their parents or by society, to seek or initiate contact with men to nearly the same degree that men were; such forthright behaviour was generally considered "unladylike."[7] This was unfortunate, since the men of the region seem to have been rather shy as well. Nor could women (or men, for that matter) easily turn to friends and relatives for companionship, since in many cases these had been left behind, sometimes far behind.

What this all added up to was intense loneliness and an almost desperate desire to find a partner, or at least to correspond with a member of the opposite sex. In the early years of the column it was not unusual for women to receive fifty letters from men in response to their published letters. So great was the volume of correspondence motivated by sheer loneliness that even the magazine's editor was compelled to comment. "Our editorial heart is truly torn with pity," he wrote in 1906, "as each mail brings us in such piteous tales of loneliness from Western maids and bachelors. We are endeavouring to carry out the wishes of our correspondents as well as possible, and are sparing no pains to put them in touch with a suitable member of the opposite sex."[8]

That so many young Canadians chose to seek a partner through a newspaper column is a further measure of their extreme loneliness; women felt the unconventionality of choosing this route even more deeply, since at the time it was still considered improper for women to take the initiative in finding a male companion, let alone advertise for one through a magazine. This explains the almost apologetic tone of some of the letters that follow and also the greater tendency of lonely maids to ask for correspondents of *either* sex and to downplay the romantic intent of their letters.

As the population of the West increased, and as towns became more numerous and accessible, the problem of lonely men and women declined. Writing from Moosomin, Saskatchewan, in 1914, one woman observed that "there are not many bachelors around here. Although they were numerous a few years ago,... they are nearly all married now and settled down nice and comfortable. Isn't it wonderful how quickly these prairies settle up?"[9] As well, a kind of backlash against the "lonesome howl," as one writer put it, began to develop at this point. Correspondents started telling bachelors to stop their whining and offered more prosaic ways of alleviating loneliness. By the war years, therefore, the number of lonely bachelors and maids writing to the Correspondence column had trailed off considerably.

But they did not disappear entirely. The war produced its own forms of loneliness, both at home and in the trenches, as the letters from "Far Overseas," and "A Lonely Westerner" suggest. And it is also clear from the letter written by "Yankee Canuck" that the war left some veterans unwilling to return to their former lonely existence and more aggressive in seeking female companionship. One might say the same of Canadian women. By the early twenties the number of lonely single women soliciting male correspondents had increased noticeably. While the reason for this is not entirely clear, it may be that women were also feeling more confident and assertive after the war, a product of their patriotic wartime efforts, their successful struggle for the right to vote, and the more liberal attitudes toward women in the postwar years.

LETTERS

May 1906
Ontario

Editor,
I am an English girl, out here [in Ontario] and often very lonely, but
see no prospects of anything better, for I never have an opportunity of
meeting any men who might possibly grow to like me. I have heard
that in the Nor'West there are many of my countrymen living isolated lives because of being so far removed from settlements, and I am
wondering if among them there may not be one in similar circumstances to myself that is suffering from loneliness and longing for a
congenial friend and comrade. If there is such a man, on ranch or
farm, who is well bred, educated, and possessed of good principles and
steady habits, I wish he would write to me in care of this column. I
will describe myself fully to him if he does, but here let me say I am
really a refined and nice girl, and as an excuse for this most unconventional proceeding on my part I plead my loneliness....
Jane Eyre

October 1906
Milestone, Saskatchewan

Editor,
... Some of the girls write and rate us bachelors for drinking and gambling, but you know nothing of the loneliness of this big country at
times, so that we are almost forced to anything to make us forget. I
often think that if you could hold out a sisterly hand to a faltering
brother it would go a long way towards steadying us, and I know at
times most of us want steadying. Now in conclusion I would say I am
a lonely bachelor and if some of you ladies would take the trouble to
write me a line or so sometimes I am sure I would be grateful.
Milestone

March 1907
Riverview, Saskatchewan

Editor,
... It touched me when Milestone said we should hold out a sisterly
hand to a faltering brother. Yes, that is what they need, not harsh criticism. Oh girls, if you could but see these 'boys' alone in their shack

on the plains and feel their utter loneliness at times you would judge more tenderly. Just try to fancy them your own brothers out there on the prairie! I have lived on the plains for over three years and have felt some of the desperate loneliness of it myself. We meet splendid people out here. They are industrious, intelligent, neighbourly and polite and we long for congenial company and someone in whom we can confide. This is my experience....

Myra

February 1908
Balcarres, Saskatchewan

Editor,

... I am an Eastern girl who has been taken up root and branch and transplanted in the glorious West three years ago. I think Eastern girls, and Western girls, too, should never lose a chance to correspond with those lonely bachelors. Just think of a man living off by himself for months at a time without hearing the sweet voice of a woman. He comes in tired and sad, there is no one to cheer him; he gets his own supper and goes to bed. This is repeated month after month. Hence I say Eastern and Western maids should never fail to send a word of cheer to these young men who are building up a glorious country that shall one day stand first among nations....

Happy Thought

March 1908
Saskatchewan

Editor,

... I am a Western farmer bachelor myself, 30 years of age, and have been farming on the prairies for the last five years, so know what the batch means. Picture to yourself, for instance, a young man alone on the prairie; his work keeps him on the homestead all the week: this is, if he attends to his duties as he should do to make a success, for the farm is a hard, though pleasant, boss—harder than most employers, with no one to talk to or confide in, unless it be his neighbours, and they generally are in the same position as himself. How he would look forward to mail day, knowing that it would contain letters from ... different parts of the country, giving him an account of themselves, their pleasures and doings, describing scenes and places. Why, it takes him out of himself for the time being, makes him forget his lonely lot, and with the knowledge that others have an interest in him, especially if it is feminine....

Miles Standish

November 1908
Saskatchewan

Editor,
... I thought I would write to pass a lonely hour away. I pity the poor
bachelors out here who have no one to talk to when they come in from
a day's work; it certainly must be lonesome for I am lonesome as I have
not been out here from the east very long.... I would like to get a letter from the fellow who calls himself 'White Pine' in your January number, or any one wishing to write. I will answer all letters with pleasure....
A Lonely Widow

February 1909
Arcola, Saskatchewan

Editor,
... How a lonely one's heart goes out to the fair writers of those dainty
letters in your pages. Some of them appeal all the more strongly from the
very naïveté of the spirit that prompted them to write. Now, girls, here's
your opportunity. It would be a charitable act to cheer up a lonely soul,
so get out your pens and paper and write me a letter. I will answer
promptly. I have a good home here, but it's a lonely task keeping house
as a bachelor, and in this district girls are conspicuous by their absence....
'A Wild Manitoba Rose' suggests that we should not be lonely, but write
to our lady friends down East; but supposing, Miss, that you know not a
single soul, man or woman down East. What then? Pray, Miss 'Wild
Rose,' write to me, then I could follow your instructions, and gladly too.
Pipe Dream

March 1909
Viscount, Saskatchewan

Editor,
... I think your correspondence department a great help to lots of the
young people. Correspondence will bring one in touch with another, as
otherwise half the men and women are too bashful to speak to each other.
There are lots of young men and women who would get married right
in our Western country only for being too backward in going forward. We
young men so seldom get in the company of young ladies that when we
do we feel too bashful to get down to business. I know that all I lack
myself is a companion to share my trials and troubles. I have been batching four years and I think that plenty long enough for any man to live
alone. The only friend I have is my violin which always stays with me.
Royal Homesteader

This unmarried teacher from Alberta's Rumsey district, c. 1920, would have felt the loneliness of her circumstances just as strongly as the typical bachelor farmer, especially if she was new to the district. Glenbow Archives/NA-2468-24

July 1909
Alberta

Editor,
… Now boys and girls, here is someone who wants correspondents, wants them badly. I am a very lonely individual and often do I feel sad and melancholy and it would be a real act of Christian kindness were you to write to me. I am living in a very lonely part of the country, at least I find it lonely, and would be pleased to receive letters or post cards from anyone, and will do my best to answer…. Boys, if you want to know what I am like just write and find out, but remember this is only for fun, as I am not on the marriage market, although the right one come along I guess you know what I should do. I think one is just as apt to meet the right one in this way as in any other…. I should like to hear from 'A Happy Saskatchewan,' 'Up a Gumtree,' 'Billy Sweet,' 'Doctor Maly,' in the April issue, and also anyone else who cares to write and cheer up a lonely little dab like me….

Seldom Seen

March 1910
Brandon, Manitoba

Sir,
… I don't know how some of them [bachelors] can say they are lonely as there is always something to be done around a farm…. A bachelor as

a rule never picks anything up he can step over, throws his paper on the floor, stands at the wood pile … and throws his wood into the house, shuts the door, sits down and stews and pines. It would be far better for him to fetch in that harness that is going to rack and ruin and repair it or that binder canvas that requires mending…. All these are cures for loneliness, but yet some may go as far as to say life is not worth living without a wife to cheer the home. Shaw!! It is all rot, such fickle heart- ed fellows as 'Scotland Yet' in your October issue ought never to have left his mother's apron strings. 'Scotland Yet,' I'm ashamed of you, to think that you belong to our noble role. Why, man, 'batching' is one of the best things a man can do; it makes him a man, to love and appreci- ate a wife when he does get one and do things for her….

Not Lonely

November 1910

Sir,
… I notice all these letters come from the young, and I have been tempted to ask, is there not a middle-aged or even older man out in our vast N[orth] W[est] who is alone and at times lonely enough to care to exchange views on paper with a woman past the halfway mark and on the down-hill side of life? I am a widow, quite alone in the world, but not looking for someone to put in 'his place.' Simply after an active life; now compelled to sit and 'spin in the sun,' and often find time hanging heavy and no one to talk with on many subjects…. If such there be, my address will be found with the Editor.

Atina

May 1911
Patchgrove, Saskatchewan

Goot tay meester!… Ay hof bin de gorresbondence golumn reading 2 year und a half next Xmas und vood like von letter to wrote. Ven I sees py der baper dot some gurls iss lonesomeness in Alberta und Sask. den goes bump de bumps mine heart mit joy for den tinks me mit mine- self, maybe dot girl like me too und maype vill wrote me somedings. So den ay say here goes, und I sits me down and von letter I wrote. But dat for me bin von awful shob for mine pen all ofer der baper vants to go…. Mine head vas leetle too big und I vas so sweet as sauerkraut und abbelsauce togedder mixed…. Vo homestead I haf got too und it gets lonesomeness mit me somedimes….

Yawkob Shtraus

July 1913

Dear Editor,

… I have been a reader [of the *WHM*] for a long time now, and find great comfort in it when I am alone in the house. As I am a lonely bachelor, I would like some correspondence from the fair sex. I think that the girls could do a lot of good for a lonely bachelor, if they would just write them a few letters…. You girls do not know how lonely a man gets in the house with no one near him to speak to. Did you ever put yourself in a bachelor's place for a few moments and try it?… A great many men when they are alone think they can do what they like on a Sunday, or any other day of the week. I think that most of this is because they get so lonely at times that they think nobody cares for them at all. So don't be backward in writing, girls. I have seen some men so lonely that when you meet them they would hardly speak to you. Afterwards they would begin to talk to you for a while and get all right, and would tell you that they were nearly dead from loneliness. Now girls, 'do unto others as you would have them do unto you.'

Farmer

One of the many bachelors who called the Prairies home in the early 1900s. Glenbow Archives/NA-227-8

December 1913
Saskatchewan

Dear Editor,
… I have been a reader of your paper for a short time, and … I always take it along to the office where I am employed. I enjoy reading it there because I am so lonesome. I don't like staying in the office all the week. I like a farming life much better, but I get very few chances to go to the farm. I feel very sorry for some of those bachelors who live so far away from neighbours. It is not so bad when you have some company. If any one cares to write to a lonely girl I will answer all letters and cards at once….

Lonely Elnor

February 1914
Sandia, Saskatchewan

Dear Editor,
… I am a new settler here in a new settlement in Saskatchewan and was raised on a farm…. There are times when one feels lonely, but work and business make the lonely thoughts disappear. It is too bad a girl is not allowed to take up a homestead here in Canada. If they were, there would not be so many lonely bachelors, and as the good book says, it is not good for man to live alone; but what will they do? I have not seen a glimpse of the fair sex all summer. I have been too busy to go out visiting, and the nearest town is thirty miles, so there is not much chance of getting acquainted. But things look a little brighter now for those single fellows as the railroad will be finished this coming summer, and a person will be able to go out and come in a little quicker than by oxen.

Thirty-Two

May 1915
Alberta

Dear Editor,
… I notice several interesting letters, one from a correspondent at Matawa, Ont. This lady states in her letters that the bachelors seem lonely and oppressed. Well some may be like that, but the majority of them are lively and content with their lot. I admit that we get lonely sometimes, but not to that extent. We know, or should know, that when we go to a new part of the country away from railroads and towns, etc., that it will be lonely; therefore, it is up to us to have the old pioneering spirit, and help to improve our land, and also to help one another. The rail-

roads will soon come, schools and churches will be built, and also we will have better homes, etc. Where I am living now, we have a new railroad and a town is building. We also get a train once a week, which is a great help. It is a lot better than 40 miles to town like it used to be.

Silent Alf

May 1915
Lampman, Saskatchewan

Dear Editor,
... Much sympathy seems to be felt for the lonely bachelors of the West. What about the poor girls who have just left a home, congenial friends, plenty of amusement, and have come to sparsely settled districts, with nothing in view but the gopher burrowed trail that leads to the barren little schoolhouse? Mail comes seldom, trips to town are few and far between, and one's life is spent, out of school hours, in a crowded farmhouse, where one is fortunate to have a room to one's self, and is usually made to feel like an imposter in the family circle. 'But,' you say, 'can she not read, or spend her time sewing, or doing fancy work? Or she might help the poor, hardworking farmer's wife.' Yes, one can do the first, and sewing and fancy work are very well, but a girl who has studied all her life has no time for learning housework, so is incapable. And one gets so tired of sewing and reading! Of course, there are compensations. And life in the West is delightful in the summer. It is only in the winter one feels the awful lonesomeness of the prairie.

Just Me [schoolteacher]

October 1916
Camp Hughes

Dear Editor and Readers,
As I have been in camp today sick, I thought I would write to your valuable paper.... I have had a homestead for about a year and have a shack on it, so when we get back I will be able to go straight to the farm.... I hope some of the fair sex will drop me a line once in a while, as it is pretty lonely when one only gets mail about once a month. So if some of the young ladies would not mind writing to a soldier boy, I would be sure to write back. I am not very good at writing, not having had much schooling, but think I will make out alright when we get to Berlin. So if any young lady wants me to bring a German helmet, why, send me your name....

Far Overseas

Mounted Police constables gather in their Coutts, Alberta, barracks for Christmas dinner, 1901. Their rather sullen expressions might be due to the lack of female companionship in most of their lives. Glenbow Archives/NA-2436-4

October 1916
France

My Dear Editor,
... I would like to correspond with someone who is a reader of your paper, preferably of the feminine persuasion. It would just cheer me up to write to someone in Canada. The past few years I spent in Manitoba and Saskatchewan, and what recollections I have of good times spent out there, dancing, skating and fall suppers, filled in many of the lonely evenings. You can quite understand how we feel out here. No girls, shows, or an evening at the Orpheum! No! Nothing but war, war, war!...
A Lonely Westerner

December 1918

Dear Editor,
... I am a young farmer and have been very busy all summer as help was so scarce.... The farm is rather a lonesome place for young people, but still I find it not so bad if there are a few dances now and again. I see some are kicking at dancing in war times. Well, I think if they were in the same place as some of us boys they would think different, for often we are all alone for a week at a time, and I think they would

be glad to go to a dance if for nothing else but to talk to someone. Some may think it fun to go homesteading and baching, but I would sooner go to war than start all over again.... Many of the boys around here were tired of farming alone and enlisted, but I have stayed with it, and will do so until after the war for wheat is badly needed....

A Lonely Boy

November 1919

Dear Editor,

... Being more fortunate than a great many of my comrades, I returned [from the war] with a whole skin. The fourteenth day of May, A.D. 1919, I was ushered into civilized life (as distinguished from army life). It certainly seemed great to be free and unfettered by the shackles of militarism, but, Oh! girls, don't I find the homestead to be a lonely place after three years of high-powered double tension excitement. No wonder they are singing "How're you Goin' to Keep 'em Down on the Farm"....

Yankee Canuck

November 1919

Dear Editor,

... Unlike most of the correspondents, I am from the city. I have never lived in the country and therefore cannot say whether I would like it or not. But while I am in the city, with all its amusements, I find it very lonesome sometimes. I am at present boarding and as the evenings seem to

Barren prairie serves as the backdrop in this shot of a young, single farm girl from Springbank, Alberta, c. 1912. Glenbow Archives/NA-3204-7

hang heavily on my hands, especially in the winter time, I would be glad to hear from some of the bachelors who write to and read this page. I will answer all letters....

City Girl

October 1922

Dear Editor and Readers,
... I am a bachelor and live on a farm in central Saskatchewan. Believe me, ... a bachelor surely leads a lonesome life, but then one has to get used to a great many unpleasant things in this world. When I feel my single blessedness most is when I try my skill at some new recipes. A few times it goes all right, but other times I feel as though I want to call for help.... I am very grateful to Brown-eyed Daisy for her sympathy for us poor bachelors. Thanks also for your willingness to send us good recipes, but I do hope you will come yourself and demonstrate how they are made. Will someone please write to a lonely bachelor who never in his life has had a love affair? I will answer all letters....

Launcelot

February 1923

Dear Editor and Readers,
Here I come begging for letters like the rest to pass away the long winter evenings. We live in an awful lonely place with nothing to see but hills and bush and not even a neighbour's light at night. The valley is very pretty in the summer time, but in winter it is very dreary. We don't have many neighbours, and the visitors are mostly those who come shooting, but forget you as soon as they get back to town....Will some of you lonely bachelors write to

Chuckie

2 The Ideal Man

The letters in this section are meant to convey the qualities that readers of the *Western Home Monthly* found desirable in a man from a romantic perspective. What constituted the "ideal man," in other words? Was there even agreement on this? And did the definition change between 1905 and 1924? We are able to answer such questions because of the nature of the magazine's Correspondence column as essentially a dating agency, at least in the prewar years. To secure correspondents, men and women would invariably specify the characteristics they wanted in a potential mate, and for a short time they even addressed directly the question, "What constitutes an ideal partner?"

But even when writers were not openly seeking mates, and as the column became largely a forum for exchanging views, they still made apparent the qualities they considered desirable in a prospective spouse. This happened in two ways. The most obvious, of course, was by expressing one's views on certain characteristics in a man or woman, whether these be good or bad in the writer's opinion. The second method was more indirect. When writers described their *own* qualities—which they frequently did to attract correspondents of the opposite sex—I have assumed that they considered these qualities to be desirable, if not necessarily "ideal." This process of self-description was, after all, an important part of "selling" oneself in the romance market, of securing a partner. Writers who gave a description of themselves were not simply saying, "This is who I am, take it or leave it," but in most cases were implicitly saying, "This is who I am, and I think it is worth having, so please write."

No doubt people exaggerated as they tried to paint themselves in the best light, and more than a few writers expressed incredulity at the near-saintliness of some correspondents. But so much the better, for in their exaggeration (or outright deception, in some cases) these romance seekers were making an even stronger statement of what they considered ideal for their own sex. It seems safe to assume that when the writer describes herself or himself without apologizing for who they are—and provided the object of the letter is clearly to form a romantic relationship—the attributes listed can be seen as constituting the ideal partner as far as that person is concerned. The letters in this section, then, include those from both women *and* men who define their ideal man.

This raises another interesting question: Did men and women share the same views about what constituted the ideal man or woman? Their views could not have diverged that much or few male-female unions would have occurred. Either that or men and women were forced to make significant compromises in their expectations or beliefs for the sake of securing a partner. More likely, and as is usually the case, men and women simply found the person who came closest to meeting their ideal. But how close were these matches? How compatible, in other words, were men and women in these years?

The letters from the *WHM* provide some answers to these questions, starting with what the readers of the magazine considered to be the ideal man. The answer changes depending on the year—there was no consistent definition of the ideal man from 1905 to 1924. Before about 1910, he was first and foremost one who abstained from certain so-called vices, primarily alcohol. As the editor noted in 1906, in an unusual aside, "many young women write us that they are willing to become the helpmate to a sober and industrious young man, but they draw the line at becoming the life partner of a man who has contracted the drink habit."[1] And several other habits besides, such as smoking and chewing tobacco, although women were more willing to put up with these lesser "evils" in moderation.

In some instances, women swore off marriage altogether because of such habits, believing that, as one put it, "ninety-nine per cent of the young men one meets with nowadays are unfit companions for any honourable woman. A man who is immoral, who swears, smokes, chews tobacco, [or] drinks liquor is a moral degenerate, nothing more or less, unfit company for a swine-herd, much less a partner of a woman's joys and sorrows."[2] Other women were willing to overlook such behaviour in the belief that the influence of a loving wife would solve the problem. Either way, male correspondents understood the female aversion to intemperate ways and clearly agreed—one of the most common assurances they gave in the early years was that they were abstainers. A Saskatchewan bachelor's assertion that "I ... do not drink, smoke, or chew [tobacco], and am free of all bad habits" was typical.[3] It is not surprising that such puritanism figured so prominently in the romantic standards of both sexes. This was the era of the great "social purity" crusade to rid society of various evils, especially drinking—a particularly serious problem out West—and the readers of the *WHM*, with rare exception, clearly shared this perspective.[4]

During the prewar period, the ideal man also did not make unreasonable demands on a wife with respect to work. Chapter 6 deals with the views of men and women regarding their domestic roles while married. For now, it is enough to note that most writers agreed that the ideal man, in the case of farmers at least, was content to have his wife do mostly housework rather than heavy labour on the farm. "I want a man who would treat me as a wife and not as a slave" was a common refrain, and many male writers went out of their way to reassure, like the gentleman from Manitoba who insisted that "I would not require her to go outdoors, except for pleasure—not even for a stick of wood."[5] Related to this was the expectation, though expressed less frequently, that perfect husbands would also allow their wives enough time to pursue leisure activities, such as dancing or going for rides, preferably alongside their husbands.

Because writers in the first five or six years of the column tended to give detailed physical descriptions of themselves, one might think that how a man looked would also have counted for a great deal. But such was not the case, either then or in later years. Few female correspondents specified the physical qualities they sought in a man, and for their part, men tended to be rather self-deprecating as far as their looks went. One farmer's observation that "I am rather dark complected, 5 feet 4½ inches tall, am as ugly as sin, but will exchange photos with any girl, she to be the judge" was not uncommon.[6] There was the occasional reference to "cleanliness" and "manliness" as being desirable, but most women were far more interested in the attitudes and behaviour of potential partners than in their appearance. As one young Ontario woman put it, "all young men that don't touch strong drink and tobacco are to be praised for it. I am not so particular about their looks or the colour of their hair, etc., if they are only clean, honest, industrious, kind and good-natured."[7] Though they rarely defined it, writers sometimes also mentioned "gentlemanly behaviour" as a positive male quality, and in the early years a number of women requested male correspondents of a Protestant or "Christian" background.

The definition of the ideal man began to change by about 1910. Both sexes showed a greater tolerance for the man who indulged in habits formerly deemed vices, especially tobacco use. Men were less likely to stress their total abstinence and women less likely to expect it. This provoked a number of heated exchanges between fundamentalist types, who chided women for lowering their moral standards, and those who felt that the occasional drink, smoke, dance, or card game was harmless. By the second decade of the twentieth century, both sexes were more likely to define the ideal man as someone who enjoyed leisure activities and was somewhat self-indulgent. The fascinating letter from the young "Anglais-Francais," below, is indicative of the new standards in male perfection. Keeping in mind the strong strain of puritanism still found in the letters of both sexes, what women increasingly looked for in prospective partners after 1910—and what men increasingly promised to be—was less clean-cut and self-denying and more fun-loving and self-indulgent.

Explaining these prewar changes in the male ideal is another matter. No doubt the weakening hold of religion in an increasingly secular, prosperous, and urbanized age had some influence.[8] Perhaps the WHM's correspondents also came to realize—especially after many male writers pointed this out—that holding men to such high moral standards, especially on the western frontier, was neither realistic nor effective. The progress of western settlement may have been a factor, too. Qualities like temperance and industriousness would have been vital for success during the earliest stages of pioneer settlement. But as the economy

improved, and as the West became a more settled region, such personal attributes may not have been considered quite as necessary in men. These qualities
would have been increasingly overshadowed by those deemed more appropri-
ate to the emerging "sporting" culture of the day, such as the willingness to par-
ticipate in dancing, skating, horseback riding, and sport.[9] The spread of rinks,
playing fields, and dancehalls, plus the greater availability (and affordability) of
musical instruments and gramophones, accentuated the new emphasis on the
physically active, "fun and games"-oriented male partner. The comments of a
"bashful" twenty-year-old Manitoba farmer in 1913 capture nicely the new per-
missiveness and nascent hedonism of the immediate prewar years. "My opinion,"
he wrote, "is [that] everyone should do as their conscience tells them is right.
For my part, I dance and can see no harm in it if it is carried on properly.
Baseball and hockey are my favourite sports, but hockey is my hobby."[10]

World War One did not significantly alter the things women looked for in
a man, but it did add a new dimension: patriotism. Contributing to the war,
especially by enlisting, became a desirable quality, according to both sexes, desirable enough to put many bachelor homesteaders on the defensive. Many western bachelors, with one eye always on the marriage market, insisted that their
farming was just as important as the contributions of those who enlisted. The
letters that follow, as well as the tendency of female correspondents to request
letters from "men in khaki," suggest that men were right to feel defensive. But
they also suggest that women, particularly rural women, recognized and
applauded the bachelor farmer's patriotic contribution on the home front.
Either way, the passionate tone of the wartime correspondence and the focus on
patriotism as a desirable trait demonstrate the impact of the war on women's
expectations of potential husbands. One can only conclude that single men perceived as not doing "their bit" between 1914 and 1918 were severely handi-
capped in the romance market, despite their other qualities.

The postwar ideal of men is more difficult to pin down, partly because of
the reduced volume of correspondence in the *WHM* and partly because the
romantic intent of the writers is less discernible.[11] But several things are clear.
With the cooling of wartime passions, wartime service no longer loomed as
large in the definition of the ideal man. If the letters from "Just Guess" and
"Fault-finder," below, are any indication, wartime military service may even
have become a liability for the romantically inclined, with several writers accusing veterans of being ungentlemanly and conceited. There is a resumption and
acceleration of prewar trends. Virtually no postwar letters mention the morality of potential male partners. Instead, writers tended to emphasize the recreational inclinations of single men, how "fun" they were. Statements such as "I
am fond of a good time" and "I am very fond of all sports" were common in
male solicitations for female correspondents and seem to have met with
women's approval. The recreational preferences themselves may have
changed—more dancing, driving cars, movie-going, and picture-taking—but
the trend toward the hedonistic-male-as-ideal-partner continued.

Men and women did not differ in their views of the ideal man during this period. In the years before the war, for example, the number of women who denounced both intemperate males and husbands who expected their wives to be "slaves" was at least as high as the number of men who did the same. This also holds true for the years 1910–19 and the early 1920s, when the ideal man was redefined in less puritanical and, during the war, more patriotic terms. There were disagreements between the sexes, to be sure. In the early years men were quick to defend their sex against accusations that most men were lazy drunks; male correspondents resented the female tendency to generalize. Quite a few also criticized women of setting their standards too high. But on the central issue of what constituted the ideal male, there was consensus.

The only possible difference between the sexes concerned the issue of a man's wealth and economic prospects. Men seem to have valued this more highly, often describing their physical assets in detail—how much land and livestock they owned, if they were farmers; the net worth of their businesses, if they were small merchants; or simply how much cash they had in the bank. Some echoed the views of the bachelor farmer from Manitoba who stated, "I should never think of matrimony unless I were in good circumstances and had a home—not a shanty, but a house of which anyone might be proud—to bring my future wife to, over which to reign as household queen."[12] In other words, being self-sufficient was important to male writers. Women, on the other hand, rarely specified wealth or economic potential as a prerequisite in a partner, the letter from "Two Squashes," below, being quite exceptional. Perhaps this was considered too crass. More likely, men, having been taught that male self-sufficiency was important, simply overestimated the female concern for such things. As "Lonely Mabel" from Victoria, British Columbia, put it succinctly, "I think consideration and kindness appeals to most women far more than the almighty dollar."[13] In any case, this gender difference disappeared after about 1910, when men and women came to define the perfect husband in identical terms.

LETTERS

December 1905
Cranbrook, British Columbia

Western Home Monthly,
I have read your correspondence column for the last few months with regard to the many favourable chances afforded women to secure husbands from among the farmers on the Prairies. I have met some of these so-called farmers, many of whom live in huts and are hardly able to keep themselves, let alone keep a woman. They could keep her poor alright. Most of those chaps are seedy, chronic, pokey, old way-backs and about the only time they show a little life is when they get filled up with bad whiskey. Thanks. None of them gents for me.

Signed, A Young Widow

February 1906
Wakopa, Manitoba

Editor,
In reply to [the] young woman in last month's *Western Home Monthly.* I desire to inform her that she errs in classing all bachelors as lazy, extravagant, useless drunken creatures, who live in miserable shacks. I am considered a good looking young man, respectable and well to do with a farm home of my own, and use neither liquor, tobacco, nor profane language and there [are] many other young men in this country just like me....

A Bachelor

March 1906
Maple Creek, Saskatchewan

Editor,
... In your issue of December 1905 a young lady of Saskatoon says all the bachelors are over-fond of the bottle. This is so with a large number ... but what of those who do not drink? I know a good many fine young men in the West who are sober and working hard to make homes. Must they be classed with the rest? But I admire the young lady of Saskatoon for not being willing to throw herself away on a man who is a slave to drink....

Rancher

In the years before World War One, many single women would have enjoyed riding off into the sunset with this Medicine Hat, Alberta, ranch hand—provided he was not intemperate or too demanding with respect to farm work. Medicine Hat Archives/PC167.18

May 1906
Portage La Prairie, Manitoba

Editor,
… With regards to the Manitoba daughters setting their caps for [having a preference for] counter clerks and preachers, I think they can be excused for that, as any young woman likes to see a clean, tidy man with a boiled shirt on and white collar, while the farmers, I am sorry to say, do not give very much attention to their personal appearance. Indeed, I know some farmers who go for months without a shave or hair-cut, for reasons best known to themselves; and what is more undesirable than an unkept creature of slovenly appearance?…

Manitoba Daughter

May 1906
S——, Manitoba

Editor,
… [I] am not anxious to get married, but if I found some one who came up to my ideal I would not hesitate in going out on a ranch or farm with him…. Of course he must be young, good-looking, Protestant; he must not use liquor or tobacco….

A Jolly Girl

September 1906
Wakopa, Manitoba

Editor,
… I sympathize with 'Young Lady of Saskatoon' for having to live in a neighbourhood peopled with drunken, lazy, extravagant foreigners. I hope her stay in that locality will not be for long, but that she will marry some good, respectable bachelor farmer (a Scotchman) and live happy and forget all her peevish notions….

Bachelor Farmer No. 9

December 1906
Cottonwood, Saskatchewan

Editor,
… There are parts of the country where young men are far too fond of a glass of whiskey with the boys. Cottonwood is one of those places, I regret to say. Recently I was present at a gathering of about a hundred people, who met together for the purpose of witnessing the joining of two lives together for good or evil. At that gathering the bride's father

This Endiang, Alberta, farmer would have ranked high among the column's correspondents in the early 1900s. Most writers at the time put a premium on men who did not expect their wives to work much outside the home. Glenbow Archives/NA-2487-1

provided whiskey, and at midnight, when I asked my escort to take me home there was not one sober person in the assemblage. I find on getting acquainted with some Ontario girls that many of them do not know the effects of liquor well enough to see when a man has taken it. Why, have those girls seen less of it than we Western girls have?...

Vinca

February 1907
Swan Lake, Manitoba

Editor,
... I do not like either the liquor or tobacco habit but I would not shun a young man on account of either. If girls knew the influence they had on youths they would not act as they do but rather exercise their influence and help them to become ideal....

Irish Lassie

February 1907
Strathcona, Alberta

Editor,
... I quite agree ... that for a husband it is essential to have a man who does not use intoxicants.... With regard to chewing tobacco I object to

that for many reasons. It injures a man's health, makes his breath smell like a sewer and is harmful to his teeth. I certainly think a man is entitled to a smoke after a hard day's work, but I hate to see a man who is a regular slave to tobacco and always has a pipe stuck in his face....

One Fair Maiden of Alta.

August 1907
Arrow River, Manitoba

Editor,
... Some of the letters from the lads and lassies are very amusing but some of the lads are very hard to please in their ideas of a wife, and they are generally the ones who make the worst husbands. The woman has just as much right to consideration as the man, but she makes the mistake of putting him first. If I were looking for a husband I would want a man who would buy his bread, get his collars and shirts done up by 'Johnny China' and milk the cows himself. I don't object to feeding a few dear little chickens and growing a few flowers provided he plants the seeds and hoes the weeds. He can smoke if he likes, because if he has a pipe in his mouth he cannot talk and it will be quiet....

Peggy McCarthy

August 1907
Calgary, Alberta

Editor,
... There is a class [of men] ... out here which is eligible as far as prosperity goes, but the personal habits of these 'gentlemen' are a nightmare to the well-born and refined girl who has been accustomed to eat with people who respect the functions of knife and fork and who are cleanly and refined in person and habits. Personally, I am too fond of my profession to marry for the sake of being married, but, of course, I should be happier in a home of my own—every woman would— with the right man, who, in my case would have to be gentlemanly, honourable and with some definite occupation and an ambition to get on in it. I will not be any man's chore boy, nor do I want to marry a moral or physical derelict such as are only too common out here. My only recommendations are good birth, the finest profession in the world, ordinary looks, youth and health....

Alice Montrose

During the second decade of the twentieth century, women looked for prospective husbands who were fond of leisure pursuits—such as these two bachelors from Olds, Alberta, out for a drive and a swim in the late 1920s. Glenbow Archives/NA-3430-11

August 1907
Baldur, Manitoba

Editor,
… If a farmer is a perfect gentleman or a true husband, he will not allow his wife to do any work outside of the house, nor will he allow her to work from morning till night, as many of them do. She should have a horse and buggy with which to go driving whenever she wished, and be able to spend her evenings driving, visiting, or playing the piano.… Valuable as the time is on a farm, I think that every farmer should take his wife for a drive in the evenings, or take her out hunting and shooting, for I have found out from my experience with the gentler sex that they never objected when asked to accompany me on a hunting or fishing expedition.…

Canadian Jack

September 1907
Saskatchewan

Editor,
… I think the girls who are opposed to smoking are quite right in their judgements. I am full of admiration for the young ladies with spunk enough to stick up for their rights, for it is their right to tell what they think in regard to men that smoke and chew, and spit that

vile, ill-smelling weed around the house, or the man who becomes lower than the lowest of animals by drinking that deadly, that abominable stuff that robs mothers of their sons, ruins and embitters the lives of noble women by the inebriation of their husbands—that stuff we were told to touch not, taste not, handle not, namely, alcohol....

Merry Sunshine [male]

December 1907
Moore Park, Manitoba

Editor,
... Our ideal man must be tall and handsome, very affectionate and with plenty of money. No farmers or counter jumpers [store clerks] need apply for us, as nothing less than a banker, lawyer, conductor or an engineer can get us. We would like an auto as a mode of conveyance, but if our ideals prefer a nice rubber-tired buggy and a spanking team of drivers, that will suit us just as well....

Two Squashes

April 1908
Hedley, British Columbia

Editor,
... Some of our lady correspondents can use the pen almost as deadly as others do the broom handle: that is, when it comes to giving bachelors a hard hit in their way through the correspondence columns. Well, probably they are giving a great many of us our just dues. But say, ladies, you can't expect to find very many angels while you have your feet on this old world of ours. Neither can you expect to find many saints riding broncos through the bunch grass, so you might as well give up the notion of looking for them....

Prospector

April 1908
Toronto, Ontario

Editor,
... Am a stenographer in Toronto and well-educated.... Personally, I think a man with a bad temper infinitely worse than a man who smokes and find that an inveterate smoker seldom has any other vices. The kind of correspondent I would like to have would be between twenty and thirty years old, tall, muscular, good natured, humorous, and all around good company—fond of sports, dancing and a good card player...

Shy Ann

August 1908
Williston, Alberta

Editor,

… I would like to meet some of those divine creatures, who don't seem to have a sin amongst the whole bunch. I bet they are that homely their faces would stop a clock. Probably their only sin was being born at all. I daresay half of these girls who say they wouldn't marry a man who drank, chewed, smoked, swore or played cards would jump at the opportunity if any of us who are addicted to these awful habits would give them half a chance. Mind you, I don't hold with a man going on a 'tear' or turning a house into a spittoon, but I certainly don't think it is going to hurt anyone quenching his thirst with a glass of beer, or taking a chew or smoke when he feels like it…. Swearing is certainly a bad habit, but no man with any gentlemanly instinct at all would think of using bad language before a lady, and what the ear don't hear, well, the heart needn't grieve over….

Flymo

May 1910
Newfoundland

Sir,

… My ideal man does not smoke, drink or play cards. He is manly, clean minded, truthful and a lover of wholesome fun. You see, I do not advocate a mummified specimen of the male sex. He must not be a fossil by any means…. Now I'm not particular about my future husband's

These two friends from Lethbridge, Alberta, c. 1916, typify the ideal in male perfection that emerged after 1910—relaxed, fun loving, and mischievous. Glenbow Archives/NA-4465-7

personal appearance; let him have the qualities aforesaid. I don't care a straw what colour his eyes are or his hair, either. He must not be perfect or remarkably handsome as it would be too much of a contrast....

A Jolly Newfoundlander

August 1910
Saskatchewan

Sir,

... I came from England nearly three year ago. I have 320 acres (homestead and pre-emption) of rolling land well suited for mixed farming. I have done my homestead duties and put in two years of my time towards getting my patent. I owe a little money but have good prospects and hope to pay all off and be clear after next harvest. I have five horses, implements &c., a comfortable two-roomed shack and barn for six head, but I am very lonely and would work with better heart and greater contentment had I a refined companion to take an interest in me and my works, and assist me as only a good woman can....

Lex

March 1911
Balcarres

Sir,

... My tastes are varied and contradictory, so in the list, my dear unknown, you will probably find something that agrees with your own, and that would form a bond of sympathy between us. Are you a good sport? Well, so am I. I can ride, drive, skate, play tennis or hockey. I can run your motor-car too, if you have one. If you haven't, you will get one because we are going to prosper. Are you fond of social life? So am I. I play cards and love to dance. "We'll two-step through life," if you like. I like to go to theatres, too, and I know how to act at an afternoon tea. Perhaps you are fond of reading and of quiet evenings at home. Well, I can imagine nothing more pleasant. You in your big armchair beside the hearth ... and I in my low rocker with my fancy work. You will read to me, or I will read to you, as you rest and smoke too, if you wish to....

Honeybunch

July 1911
Leifur, Manitoba

Sir,
Say, Hello, girls! Now, just a minute, look here, I'm not one of those guys who does not swear, nor smoke, nor chew. I can do all, having learned the theory in the city and the practical use of each since I came to the homestead. Believe me, girls, I am a peach—especially at chewing—anything that's good to eat....

Brown Eyed Solitaire

July 1911
Switzer Jct., Manitoba

Dear Editor,
... Now my choice for a man is a good-looking fellow. He must be a good size, so if he ever gets thin, he won't have to stand twice in the sun to leave a shadow; he almost must dance, play cards ... and be able to go out every evening in the week and church on Sunday and not say he is very tired every Sunday. His habits must be modern, he can smoke all the treat cigars he gets, but must not buy any himself, he can drink once in a while as long as he does not get completely drunk, he must get full on nothing but ice cream and soda water, and must be in early two nights a week. Now, boys, I am not hard on you, for lots of women would not let you out alone. Ha, ha!...

Browney

February 1912
Calgary, Alberta

Dear Editor,
... You know, I am one of those young fellows that believe in "having a good time," as we are only going through this world once, and so don't want to miss anything that's good.... I don't care for smoking, but it's great to show off with an Havana cigar occasionally. Dancing, why I am never so happy as when I feel myself waltzing through the air to the strains of the 'Blue Danube,' etc. I was very straight laced and religious once, but time slips around, for "we are only poor weak mortals after all";... some papers and books and periodicals are full of good advice and right living; but, after all these exhortations, there isn't much "bucking up" to the standard, and the world goes on just the same.... I suppose some readers will imagine I'm one of those "fast ones." Well, I must say, I hope I'm not that bad yet, although I believe in having a good time, and being jolly, and trying to make life worth

living.... I think the average man or woman knows when they are going too far, and it's up to them to assert their will power and see what they are made of....

Anglais-Francais

April 1912
Whitebeach, Saskatchewan

Dear Editor,
... I think physical culture is a very important thing. Some of us get this in our employment, and are growing up with manly farms and strong arms. But there are others in the city who are coming up delicately with spindle shanks, and narrow shoulders, wand flat chests, and weak arms—great babies, with soft hands and soft muscles, and not enough physical prowess to under take to carry a disputed point with the cook in the kitchen. How a woman ever makes up her mind to love such a man as this is a mystery to me. A feminine man is a masculine monster, and no woman with unperverted instincts can love and marry him. A true woman loves a pair of good strong arms, fastened to a pair of broad shoulders, for they can defend her, and provide for her....

H. P. [male]

March 1914
Carstairs, Alberta

Dear Editor,
... As the topic of an ideal person is now being discussed and "Western Sun" wishes a picture of an ideal man, we will give the description which appeals to us. We do not think his age or the colour of his hair (although we prefer dark hair) has anything to do with the person. A tall, well-built manly man with dark hair, a good character, ambitious, free from the use of tobacco and liquor; a man of refinement and who is not afraid to offer a hand to raise the fallen and has a cheery word for everyone. We do not think it necessary for anyone to be a church member and take much interest in the work....

Kate and Duplicate

July 1915
Keefers, British Columbia

Dear Editor,
... "Thistle" has invited some one's opinion on the subject of patriotism.... I think there should be two classes of patriots, the one that goes and fights at the front and one that stays at home and goes about with

a cheerful manner, doing his work the same as if there was no war at all. Some people seem to have an idea that the men who stay at home are cowards. This is right enough in some cases, but I want to know what would happen to this country if every able-bodied man were to leave everything behind him and go to the front.... If all the farmers were to throw down their tools and all went to war, where would the food supply of both soldiers and civilians come from?...

R. M. R.

June 1916
Alberta

Dear Editor,
I see that most of the correspondents have a good opinion of the bachelor homesteaders, but there are some inclined to think that they are a little lower than the ordinary.... Now they talk about the hero of war, but I think a young man that will leave a comfortable home and come out here to pave the way for others is just as big a hero as the others.... Now around here there are 15 bachelors. Out of the 15 there are only 2 who drink to my knowledge and 5 who smoke; 3 of them have enlisted, so I think if the bachelor homesteaders are the same all over as they are here they are a little higher, not lower than ordinary....

Homesteader

A willingness to don the khaki and fight for one's country was an indispensable quality for the romantically inclined Canadian bachelor between 1914 and 1918. Glenbow Archives/NA-3419-3

July 1916
Alberta

Dear Editor and Friends,
... I see in the February number where someone sprung a new topic for discussion—'What have I done'[for the war]... I have done what I could in supporting Red Cross work, I have donated a brother to the army, and a little over three years ago I filed on my half section.... My land raised over a thousand bushels of wheat last year and my earnest intentions are to grow more wheat to make more flour to help feed more soldiers. I was interested very much in the letters by "Prairie Nurse" and "B.C. Field Flower."...

Progressive

July 1916
Saskatchewan

To the Readers,
I have spent many evenings reading the *W.H.M.*, and always find it good reading.... That poor bashful fellow of 29 years of age who has gone with a girl for eleven years, and can't find courage enough to propose to her, sure had my sympathy. Poor soul, why doesn't he enlist? [T]he ladies will run after him so much, he will be glad to propose to one to get rid of the others....

Ameysth

September 1916
Okotoks, Alberta

Dear Editor,
... In the June issue I very much enjoyed "Homesteader's" letter.... I can realize how hard it must be to do your own work outside, then come in and do your housework. But now that you have such a good start, do not give up. Luck will come your way. As you said, homesteaders do not get the credit that is coming to them. Most of us can praise the soldiers who go and fight for us, but no word for the men who work from morning till night to feed us....

Farmer's Girl

February 1917

Dear Editor,
... I know many girls who did not agree with young farm boys enlisting; later, when their own brother enlists, they think every man ... no

matter what they are doing, should be wearing khaki, simply because their brother is doing so. It is ridiculous for some girls to say they would not be seen with a civilian and "He ought to be wearing khaki." Of course, there are exceptions, but there ought to be a decided difference made between the boys and men doing their bit on the farm and the real "shirker." Boys under twenty-one (I think) are physically unfit and are better at home helping the Empire here.... I have many soldier friends, all of whom I esteem very highly, and some of them would be doing their bit had they remained at home.... As for the class of girls referred to, they are certainly shallow-minded, and are not deep enough to take the matter seriously as to the man's duty.... The Allies have to be fed, and is it not our farmers who are doing it?...

Spitfire [female]

March 1917

Dear Editor,

... I see that none of you girls speak about dancing. I am a dancer from my little toe to the top of my head.... We have dances in our school every two weeks, and the last one was a good one. There were over 100 people and half of them were girls. These girls all come from the towns and say we have a good time too. I suppose some of you girls will say "He is some old fellow who is gone in the head." But, say, girls, I'm not. I am one of the young fellows off the farm who do not smoke or chew tobacco or use liquor of any kind, so don't be afraid, girls. I am a farmer's son and full of fun....

Sky-Scraper

April 1917

Dear Editor,

I cannot resist answering 'Spitfire'.... I, too, know girls who do not agree with farm boys enlisting. Thank goodness they are getting few and far between. You never hear a girl or a family who have any loved ones there talk like that, and I presume by her letter she has no brother there.... I would not be seen with a civilian unless he wore the rejection button or had a reasonable excuse for being here. I say thank God our brave young lads went. Where would we be today had we waited for older ones alone to fill the ranks. Every boy in khaki is a hero in my sight.... No, it isn't for us to tell men to go, but it's our duty to show them theirs and help them to go.... I would like to hear from any khaki lads....

Pocahontas

June 1917

Dear Editor,
I have just read the correspondence in the *Western Home Monthly* for April and the letter by "Pocahontas" has got "me going." I do not think that she knows about farming, or she wouldn't say that any other business is just as important in this stage of the world's history. Barring munitions, farming is the one thing that is winning this war today, and a boy is more good on the farm than he would be in the trenches (by boys I mean ones under eighteen years of age).... I do not have any brothers at the front, but I have uncles and cousins. I will not hide behind their loyalty however. I am seventeen years of age, and my brother and I have all the work on the farm to do ourselves.... I would like to see another letter from "Pocahontas".... She is likely to call me a slacker or something of that kind, but it's worth it.

A Mere Boy

August 1917

Dear Editor,
... By the way, I admire the sailor lads as much as the soldiers. They are doing as much and perhaps more than the khaki lads; but I hear little in praise of them from our corner. Perhaps because the khaki is more becoming. Personally, I think some of the young ladies think more of the looks of a suit of khaki than of the thing it stands for. The uniform is what gets their eye....

Bonehead [male]

September 1917

Dear Editor,
... I am a young farm girl and have lived on the farm all my life, so I hardly agree with "Pocahontas" about farm boys enlisting.... Pocahontas also says that she would not be seen with a civilian unless he had reasonable excuse for being here. I went to a picnic the other day and there were no solders there, they were all young men without any excuse for not being at the front, only they are farmers. "Pocahontas" will likely call them all "slackers" because they did not enlist. I agree with "Irish Nora" about young men being called "slackers" by the young girls, but I think it is mostly the city girls who call them "slackers."...

Sunshine

November 1917

Dear Editor,
… I quite agree with "Pocahontas." If we had all stayed at home we would
soon not have had any farms to work on. I myself left the farm and enlisted. I lived out in Western Manitoba … but I thought it my duty to enlist.…

Scott

P.S. Would like to hear from any of the members, especially
"Pocahontas."[Note: she wrote back, in November, "Please forward
enclosed letter to 'Scott.' I'm indeed glad someone understood me."]

July 1920

Dear Editor and Readers,
… I should like to hear your opinion of the modern young man.… It
seems to me that the returned boy [veteran] has been made a great
deal of—and justly so—but has the attention he has received gone to
his head a tiny little bit? Of course, "The more one has, the more one
wants." With apologies if I have offended anyone.

Del [female]

September 1920

Dear Editor and Readers,
… Being a farmer's son, I find enough things during the day to attend
to than to think of loneliness.… I join in all kinds of sport, but like
baseball and hockey best. I do not dance much myself, but I have nothing to say against the useful exercise of dancing as it proves to be to
those who sit all day at one kind of work.… My brother and I go to
dances just for the reason of providing good music for the entertain-
ers. We play the clarinet and cornet to the best of our ability.… I like
farming in Manitoba very much.… We have about ten acres of potatoes this year and have been using new potatoes from the 5th of July.…
I have a Hudson Super Six-cylinder car and I would like Cupid to
help me find a fair chauffeur with or without experience. I am nineteen years old, 5 ft. 10 ins. high and weigh 168 lbs.…

Steve

October 1920

Dear Editor and Readers,
… I think 'Del' has voiced my thoughts exactly. "The attention given
the returned soldier has gone to his head," and I think more than a

Two bachelors motorcycling in Calgary in 1913 typify the fun-loving men that women corre-spondents were beginning to prefer at this time. Glenbow Archives/NA-2667-2

little. True they have done much for us. The modern young man, or the most popular modern young man, is far from my ideal, and I am sure from yours, dear readers, if you only go into your hearts for your real feelings. What is the cause of all this careless, boisterous, low and lazy life the average young man is living? In almost every case it is his parents' fault.... The trouble in most cads began when he was a very little boy. Just stop and recall the homes you have entered. I can say that out of every hundred you visit in Canada today five per cent only have children who respect and obey their parents and elders and are well mannered.... Five per cent of all the young men in Canada in a very few years, as it is today, will be worthy the name of a gentleman....

Just Guess [female]

December 1920

Dear Editor and Readers,

... "Just Guess" has ridden rough-shod over the popular young man and I quite agree with her in most things she says.... There is just one thing; she blames the parents too much I think.... I think, "Just Guess," that you forgot to mention the more rough and ready he is the more careless and useless he becomes and the girls fall right in line with him. So just as long as there is that kind of a girl there will be that kind of a young man....

Fault-finder [male]

March 1921

Dear Editor and Readers,

... I am very fond of reading at which I spend [a] great deal of my spare time. I like other sports such as skating and dancing ... I have a small kodak which takes very good snaps. Perhaps I could exchange some with "Primrose No. 2" as she seems very interested in photography....

Smiling Bachelor

October 1921

Dear Editor and Readers,

... Have just been reading the *W.H.M.* and see that "Happy 4th" is asking for exchange of snaps. I have a 2½ x 4¼ camera and would be delighted to exchange snaps with him, also Smiling Bachelor if he would like to do so. Was looking over some back numbers of the *W.H.M.* and saw a letter from Patches. Poor boy, I would like to help you wash the dishes and help you push 'Lizzie' out of the snow drifts. "Cheerio," [I] remember you well and would like to correspond with you, only you must write first. I also thought "40 Bachelor" in the December issue wrote a fine letter and if he cares to write to a lover of all nature and animals, I will answer him. My favourite pastimes are horseback riding and dancing....

Sammy [female]

April 1923

Dear Editor and Readers,

... I am a Yankee, came here two and a half years ago.... I have done all kinds of work and have lived in big cities and in small towns both in U.S. and in Canada. One can have a good time in the city if they have plenty of money; if not, the farm is the best. One can live happily wherever he goes if he has the right disposition. A country is what the people make it. I enjoy myself wherever I go. I play, sing, dance, play cards, also go to church and enjoy it all. Now I am not sweet sixteen, have seen twice that and a little more, but I can enjoy myself just as much as those at sixteen and can get around just as fast. I live in Central Saskatchewan and it is very fine in the summer. If any of the fair sex would care to write I promise to answer all letters....

Yankee Doodle Boy

3   The Ideal Woman

Contributors to the *Western Home Monthly's* Correspondence column spent as much time—if not more—defining what constituted the ideal Canadian woman as they did the ideal Canadian man. And they did so in the same ways. Either they noted the desired attributes in the letters of men seeking female partners, or they revealed them indirectly, through the self-descriptions of women hoping to attract male interest. The same questions arise from any analysis of these views: Is it possible to identify a single stereotype of the ideal woman? If so, did this stereotype change between 1905 and 1924? And were there any differences between the sexes in defining this stereotype?

The first thing that becomes apparent is that while a single stereotype of the ideal woman is discernible, it is much broader than in the case of the ideal man; this is particularly true for the years before World War One. Men simply had to abstain from certain vices and place few demands on their wives outside of housework to be considered desirable, but women had to be so much more. Most importantly, they had to be willing to work hard, at least if they planned to marry a western farmer. Many male correspondents do little to conceal their contempt for the lazy young woman whose only interest was in living an idle life of recreation and material consumption and who, as a result, preferred well-off city men over struggling bachelor farmers. "Nowadays," wrote one "disgusted" fellow from Manitoba, "young women want to start in life just where papa left off, with palatial residences, horses, carriages, servants, etc.," so that "the man who can bid the highest secures the would-be prize."[1] Another complained that "all the girls up here [Saskatoon] are senseless creatures without a single accomplishment. They think of nothing but dress and society."[2] If intemperance was the most undesirable male quality in these early years, laziness, especially if accompanied by lack of thrift, was certainly the least favoured female one.[3]

The many single farmers who wrote to the *WHM* wanted a woman who would work hard to make a good home, who would, in essence, be a good "housekeeper." Apart from their constant loneliness, men were clearly tired of having to carry the double burden of starting a farm and keeping house. After a long day working in the fields, they wanted a neat and tidy home and a hot meal to return to. Housekeepers with farm experience, strength, and good health were especially desirable, since they could, if required, help out with chores, such as milking cows and caring for poultry. But men were quick to point out—as noted in the previous chapter—that they would require such assistance only on rare occasions, as when the men were away from the farm for extended periods. The large number of women who boasted of their abilities to keep a clean house and cook a decent meal, or who cited their farm experience, suggests that many women also considered good domestic skills an important prerequisite for securing a husband.

But men wanted more than just housekeepers and helpmates. In the prewar years they also wanted a companion, someone to talk to and spend leisure time with, someone to share their hardships and joys. Even nonfarmers wrote that the ideal woman was someone whose company they could enjoy. What made for a good companion is another matter, but men often defined this as someone who was cheerful, encouraging, loving, fairly well-educated, and optimistic. Bachelor farmers in particular would have found these qualities desirable given the demands and uncertainties of their work and their fragile morale, especially in the early years of settlement.

A number of writers sought wives of "refinement," who could sing or play the piano, and wives who enjoyed certain leisure pursuits, such as riding and dancing. It is interesting to note how many women advertised their musical abilities and education as assets. On the whole, one might say that men wanted partners with the stamina and skills of country-bred women and the education and cultural refinement of city-bred women.

Religion was the third female quality that many writers prized during these years. It is remarkable to see so many men asking for either "Protestant" or "Christian" wives and in some cases specifying that "no Catholics need apply." This was perhaps understandable since most of the men who wrote to the journal were Protestant. What is less clear is why the ideal woman was so frequently defined in such religious terms when the ideal man was not, except indirectly. This likely had something to do with the commonly held view that women were the main repositories and defenders of moral virtue, that they were responsible for imparting and spreading Christian values.[4] What man would settle for a woman who took this responsibility lightly, especially if he planned to start a family or if he too was in need of some "civilizing" influence? Women must have understood this, for they often noted their religious affiliations in their letters. The only other "ethnic" criterion that occasionally appeared in the letters was the preference—even among recent immigrants from the United Kingdom—for "Canadian" girls, as opposed to "English" girls in particular. Men probably believed that Canadian girls were less afraid of hard work and had more farm experience too.[5]

The ideal woman in the prewar years was also more likely to be defined in terms of her age and physical appearance than was the ideal man. Men usually solicited letters from "young" women (younger than themselves at any rate) of a particular hair and eye colour, complexion, height, even weight, and they often specified that their prospective partners must be "good looking." Male tastes were too varied to allow for any generalization regarding physical preferences, but "red heads" and women with freckles were definitely unpopular across the board. Such physical criteria stemmed in part from practical concerns—namely, a desire to marry someone healthy and hardy enough to handle life on a farm—and women did their best to reassure in such cases. "Some of your correspondents seem to think that weight is a necessary qualification for a wife," wrote one farmer's daughter from Manitoba. "I am a very healthy girl and have had a great deal of outdoor life with the result that I am rather fat," by which she likely meant stout.[6] In other cases, of course, men were concerned purely with the aesthetic. In most instances, though, cosmetic considerations

This sturdy and cheerfully disposed Calgary woman doing her laundry outdoors represents perfectly the "ideal woman" of the early 1900s. Glenbow Archives/NA-4910-10

took a back seat to less tangible female qualities, which might explain why so few men requested photographs from prospective partners and why so few women offered to send them.

Overall, the ideal female partner in the early years of the column—from 1905 to about 1912—was defined as a hard-working, competent housekeeper and helpmate, an amiable, educated, fun-loving companion, a committed Protestant, preferably native-born, and a young, sturdy, good-looking woman, in that order. One twenty-six-year-old Alberta man summed up the ideal well: "I want a healthy, refined, educated Christian wife, with musical talents and a cheerful, lively, fun-loving disposition; good looking, well built, and a good cook and housekeeper."[7] This general preference would also explain why female schoolteachers had such a bad reputation among bachelors—"school ma'arms," as they were called, were thought to possess few of these qualities.

This ideal slowly changed over time, starting around 1913. First of all, men made less of the domestic abilities of potential wives and more of their recreational inclinations. "We prefer city girls, those that sing or recite," wrote "Sammy and Pal," two bachelors from Manitoba, "as we do not intend our wives to be household drudges."[8] Nor, increasingly, did women wish to be so. "We are all fond of music," declared three young women from Alberta, "and can play and sing. We are very fond of sports, such as skating, riding, etc., can cook and keep a tidy home *if need be*.[9] Few correspondents were this blunt, but their messages, and the new standard in female perfectibility they symbolized, were clear enough. This explains the strong and persistent backlash from members of both sexes who criticized writers for undervaluing domestic abilities and playing up leisure abilities. The lively exchange between "23, Skidoo" and "A Homestead and Bachelor Boy," below, illustrated the tensions that accompanied the slightly revised ideal of a female partner during the second decade of the twentieth century. The ideal woman, like the ideal man, became more hedonistic in the immediate prewar years, and not everyone was happy about it.

By the years 1910–19, as well, men placed less emphasis on religion and physical appearance. Men, almost abruptly, stopped making "Protestantism" a prerequisite, and both sexes began criticizing the tendency of earlier writers to provide physical descriptions of their desired mate or of themselves. "I am certainly amused at the way some of the young people describe themselves," wrote "A Lonely Bachelor" from Saskatchewan in 1912. "The way they describe their height, weight and good looks, you would think it was a bronco they wanted to sell."[10] The changing nature of the Correspondence column—which became less a matrimonial bureau and more a forum for simply voicing opinion— might account for the decreased emphasis on physical appearance. But there does appear to have been a genuine rethinking of looks as an important quality in the prospective wife. The changing role of women in Canadian society may have had something to do with it. As women became more prominent in the workforce, dressed more casually, and fought publicly for social reforms, society may have come to value them less for their ornamental qualities and more for their substance. Certainly their wartime efforts would have contributed to this shifting view of what made for a desirable wife.[11]

But concern about physical appearance did not disappear altogether. In 1914 and 1915 several correspondents commented with disapproval on the growing tendency of women, particularly in urban areas, to wear makeup and flashy clothes. Even in the early years, male writers sometimes expressed a preference for the woman who dressed simply, although this was largely a financial concern, as struggling farmers did not want their hard-earned money spent on "dresses and gowns fit for a queen."[12] On the other hand, the deafening silence of most correspondents on the issue of female comportment seems to say a lot more, namely that the new trends were increasingly condoned. Indeed, if the scathing letters from "Freda" and "Alfred the Second" in this chapter are accurate, men greeted the new styles with wholehearted approval. It is possible that in the years approaching World War One, the ideal woman was increasingly defined as the "made up" or "modern" woman who fussed over herself and dressed alluringly. "Ideal" is perhaps too strong a word in this instance, especially in the context of the war, when many Canadians likely frowned on such ostentation. The shortage of male letters during the war makes it difficult to draw firm conclusions either way, but the ideal woman from 1913 to 1918 seems to have been someone in between the sensibly dressed, austere woman of former years and the heavily "powdered" and "painted" "street-walker" type usually associated with working-class city girls.

Perhaps in response to the growing importance that women placed on appearances, a number of men writing to the column after 1912 further expressed a preference for women who did not judge a man by his clothes. Women took up much space defending their sex against charges that they were reducing the measure of a man—especially the rural man—to whether or not he wore overalls. In the end both men and women agreed that the ideal woman judged a man for what he was, not what he wore.

The changes to the view of the ideal woman that took place in the years after World War One confirm the idea that the years 1910–19 were a transitional period.[13] Not only were there virtually no references to women's domestic abilities and religious affiliations, but there were also far fewer criticisms of female immodesty. Some writers, such as "Rover," below, even defended women's use of makeup. Both male and female writers seem to have embraced the modern woman, or "flapper," as she was more commonly known, as the new ideal. Male writers spoke with almost one voice in their desire to meet a woman who was open, affectionate, and fun-loving—the "jolly girl" type, who was more willing to go out with men for the fun of it, rather than as a prelude to marriage. Typical of this new sentiment was the comment by a nineteen-year-old farmer who wrote in 1920 that "in some districts the girls are taking advantage of leap year and having dances, etc. If the boys here have to wait for the girls to get up a dance we certainly would have to wait. Perhaps it is on account of the cold weather that we have had here that the girls are so 'frozen,' but we hope that when spring comes they will thaw out."[14] As this comment implies, the ideal postwar woman was fond of physical recreation. In short, by the early 1920s the perfect female partner was more outgoing—even bold—and, like her male counterpart, far more hedonistic.

The reasons for the changing ideal are not entirely clear, but the letters leave little doubt that the war was partly to blame. The brutal four-year conflict put the last nail in the coffin of many Victorian ideals, particularly religious ones. This might explain why both men and women placed less emphasis on

By the 1920s, the ideal woman was far more likely to dress casually and engage in more hedonistic pursuits, including sports. Glenbow Archives/NA-4844-37

domesticity and religion as female prerequisites. At the same time, the war bred a rebellious "live for the moment" mentality that put a premium on the fun-loving attributes of potential female partners. Soldier-veterans, whose wartime experiences made them more, shall we say, worldly, would have felt these changes even more strongly. One sees in their letters to the *WHM*, several of which are reprinted here, a desire to become acquainted with the sort of women they encountered in England and France during the war, women who were less reserved in every way.

On the whole the magazine's male and female correspondents were of one mind in redefining the qualities young Canadians considered desirable in women. But some gender differences existed. In the years before 1911, men tended to emphasize the importance of appearance more than women did (the letter from "Tomboy" being an extreme example of this), while women tend-ed to play up their domestic skills, especially their cooking. After 1911 women were more likely than men to mention their recreational preferences and, dur-ing the war especially, to boast of their ability (and desire) to handle "men's work," such as herding cattle or ploughing and harvesting, in the case of rural women. This discrepancy continued into the early postwar years, as a number of women expressed the desire to pursue unconventional careers, but by the 1920s both sexes came to define the ideal woman in almost identical terms.

The greatest difference seems to have been between rural and urban cor-respondents. Young adults in rural areas were more likely to define the ideal woman as one who could do her share of work on the farm and who took her religious responsibilities seriously. Urban correspondents, by contrast, placed the emphasis on a woman's refinement, education, and love of leisure pursuits. The comments of a twenty-one-year-old Manitoba woman in 1909 illustrate well the urban view. "I live in the city when home," she wrote, "but have been travelling or at college most of the time for the past four years.... Am very fond of art, music, skating, reading and sleeping. Can do a little house work when necessary, as I spent a term in a Domestic Science School."[15] Rural inhabitants were also more likely to idealize the modestly dressed, natural-looking woman, while urban inhabitants preferred the flamboyantly attired, "made up" one. The evidence on this score is impressionistic since the *WHM* stopped publishing the precise origins of the letters by 1914 and there has been no methodical analy-sis of rural-urban differences for the early years. But if the distinction were to hold true, it would explain some of the changes that the definition of the ideal woman underwent, in the pages of the *WHM*, as Canada became a predomi-nantly urban society between 1905 and 1924.

LETTERS

February 1906
Shelbrooke, Saskatchewan

Editor,
… Most young ladies now-a-days are looking for a snap, they are looking for a husband who could afford to keep a servant girl the year
around. I know a young woman who, before her marriage, claimed
that she was prepared to hold up her end. After she got married all she
cared for was the rocking chair. We bachelors are not looking for that
kind. I am looking for a good, sensible, working young woman.

A Farmer Bachelor

February 1906
Wakopa, Manitoba

Editor,
… Allow me to inform you that I know a number of farmers' daughters
in Manitoba who would neither marry the lonely bachelor, nor help him
to cook for his threshing hands, but would rather sit in a corner and play
the piano, or practice a dialogue for a concert, and set her cap for a counter clerk, or a preacher of the gospel. She would laugh at the bachelor
farmer across the way who might happen to not have his crop threshed,
and think that because her papa had his in the granary that he was better than the rest of us. She might think that because a bachelor farmer
was not as well off as her papa that he is green and should not have a wife.
Oh what conceit on the part of our Manitoba daughters.…

A Bachelor

February 1906
Stoetzel, Saskatchewan

Editor,
… I would gladly give any good woman a home. I care not if she be
young, strong, and good looking. I would like her to be cheerful and
kind and willing to share the lot of a humble, plain, and honest man.
I have bached for a number of years, and shall continue to do so until
I meet some young woman with more than a reputation for good
housekeeping to recommend her. I don't want simply a housekeeper.
I want a wife.

Vacuum

April 1906
Knee Hill Valley, Alberta

Editor,

… Have you any readers of your paper among the foreign class of
Protestant Christians marriageable girls—Doukhobors, Galicians,
Swedes, Danes or Norwegians—for it would appear that the girls from
England, Ireland, and Scotland here do not seem very suitable for a
farmer's wife? They like too well to sit in the rocking chair and chew
gum to be of real service to the busy farmer bachelor, who has to get
out and rustle for a living. It is my opinion that we will have to rely
on the working class of girls for wives. This class seems to be found
among the Doukhobors, Galicians, and Germans…. I am O.K., well
fixed, but I must have a wife to help me out….

Alberta Boy

April 1906
[no address]

Editor,

… A nice, plain, serviceable everyday healthy Protestant Christian
girl, between 20 and 30 years, will find it to her advantage to correspond with me. I am not a stickler as to size, beauty, wealth or
nationality. She must be honest and truthful and willing to live on
a farm in Alberta. Lazy girls, deformed cripples, cranks and
Catholics not wanted. I will be glad to hear from girls with character above reproach….

[no name]

April 1906
Lauder, Manitoba

Editor,

… I am a prosperous young farmer with a half section of land fully
equipped with horses and machinery and my ideas of a good wife run
something as follows. She should be a good cook, willing to feed and
look after the poultry, pigs, calves, milk about five cows, keep the house
clean, do the washing, ironing, weed the garden and be prepared to get
a lunch on the table for an occasional caller. Of course she could play
the piano, go to town or mend the clothes in her spare time. Hoping
you will be able to send me a photograph of a suitable young lady of
dark complexion….

A Home Lover

In the early years of the twentieth century, strength and a willingness to work hard were key attributes for single women hoping to nab a western bachelor farmer. Glenbow Archives / NA-4179-21

May 1906
Portage la Prairie, Manitoba

Editor,
... I beg leave to say a word or two in favour of the farmers' daughters of Manitoba. I think the 'Wakopa Bachelor' is very severe in his criticism of them. There are a great many good, sensible young women among them, and capital housekeepers, who can make butter, milk cows, cook for threshing hands, and look after poultry of all kinds, as well as sit and play the piano, which I think is a very necessary accomplishment for the young woman who wishes to be a cheerful and entertaining companion....

Manitoba Daughter

October 1906
Maple Creek, Saskatchewan

Editor,
I am anxious to become acquainted with some jolly go-ahead girl
who does not object to smoking and whiskey that is indulged in to
moderation. One who can make herself a bright, amusing companion
on a ranch some distance from town. She must be healthy and good
tempered, fond of outdoor pursuits (riding, shooting, etc.) and if she is
musical and a good singer so much the better.... The girl of my choice
must be well-educated, not prudish, physically perfect and able to hold
her own in any company. I want her for a wife, not a slave....

Sportsman

February 1907
Portage la Prairie, Manitoba

Editor,
You bachelors! Are you not ashamed of yourselves? So many of you
living up there in the West in solitary state and so many of us poor girls
down here in the same condition! Now, would you not like your meat
cooked for you, instead of having to cook it yourselves? When you are
tired and hungry just think of eating pie, cake, pudding, sausages and
all the other nice things a woman knows how to cook. Does it not
make your teeth water to think of it?...

One of the Lassies

February 1907
Dauphin, Manitoba

Editor,
... Grubbing roots and following the plough are my favourite occupa-
tions, and in my spare moments to play on the mouth-organ, which I
can do very well. I intend getting a banjo, so would prefer a girl who
is a fairly good musician for a partner.... I prefer black or brown hair—
no red heads need apply. She must be willing to live on a farm and help
a fellow along. I don't mean her to be a slave, but a cheerful, contented helpmate. Of course she must be a good housekeeper and cook....

Plough Boy

March 1907
Lacombe

Editor,
... In the first place I want a wife whom I can love above all other
women and who can love me more than she can love any other man,
for when love fills the heart of man and wife many an obstacle can be
overcome which might cause conflict under other circumstances. I
appreciate neatness of dress, care of toilet, witticism, cheerfulness, love
for the home, ability to sew, cook, play the piano and converse on ordinary topics of the day, and I should take pride in one that can milk a
cow if needful and handle a horse. And more than this, I regard as most
important of all a love for God and humanity....

Square Deal

April 1907
Ebor, Manitoba

Editor,
... We have lived on the farm for 8 years and are very fond of the
country. We enjoy everything to do with farming and are both well
trained in domesticity. We are of good education, musical and fond of
good literature. We are pretty Protestants and have brown hair and
eyes. We are 5 ft. 5 ins. in height and 20 years of age....

Twin Sisters

May 1907
Touchwood, Saskatchewan

Editor,
... I would like to correspond with some young ladies who are musi-
cally inclined, who have refined tastes, and are not too fond of this
world's pleasures and would give proper attention to the making of a
home. I don't want the expensive sort, but just a good everyday
respectable sort, with plenty of life and fond of harmless conversation,
not gossip or slander. I prefer a fair complexion, with either blue or
dark eyes, dark hair, fairly tall and proportionately built, of good figure, and above all, healthy and strong, with a loving disposition and
used to farm life. Must be a good cook and housekeeper.

Lonely Hopeful

July 1907
Winnipeg, Manitoba

Editor,
… What I am looking for is a small-sized girl, with blue eyes and a love for music, and who has been educated beyond the point of saying "It don't" and "Was you"….

Pharos

October 1907
Alberta

Editor,
… The girl I marry must be very high-toned and fond of buggy and horseback riding and all sorts of sports, especially dancing, as I am very fond of them myself. I pity those who have to cut out dancing on account of their wives. Of course, it is all right not to go to dances in the busy season, but during leisure months one should have a good time. Not work from daylight till dark from year to year to get a few more dollars, for one will be no better off in the year 2,000….

Smoky Mokes

December 1907
Calgary, Alberta

Editor,
… I find the letters in the correspondence columns interesting, some amusing, especially letters from those that figure as educated, refined damsels dictating their terms if they become the wife of a poor rancher in a new country…. Some of those dainty dames deserve the garret cat and parrot. Education, accomplishments, grace of form and feature are all thistledown in the shake, compared to the girl that can render you some assistance out and in for a few years until you get a little bit into shape…. How much help could a wife give a young chap starting on a farm who objected to do a chore boy's work occasionally?… Dolls in glass cases and the doukhobors hitching their wives to the plough are the two extremes and if any husky maiden fair, fat and forty cares to accept the happy medium, I shall be glad to correspond with her with a view to matrimony.

Robie Ranteltree

September 1908
Trout River, Quebec

Editor,

... I am just a tall, fair-haired, blue-eyed Irish school-marm. I guess that's enough to frighten any Western bachelor, without telling about my cooking, but here goes. I can bake potatoes and beans, but that is about all; and as for milking, the least said about that the better, but, sure, there's lots of time to learn, as I'm only eighteen. I love dancing and candy, and I like boys, too, if they are tall, good-looking and agreeable, and not red-headed....

Towhead

February 1909
Wingham, Ontario

Editor,

... I am sweet sixteen, 5 feet 4 inches tall, weigh about 109 pounds, have a wealth of golden hair, hazel eyes, pearly teeth and a fair complexion. I like lots of fun and am very fond of any kind of music; can play the piano nicely. I am also considered a very graceful dancer. I can cook a good square meal and am a good housekeeper....

Golden Locks

A husband and wife outside their log home in Vermilion, Alberta, c. 1907. Marriage was seen as a partnership, one in which wives had a substantial voice in family matters. Glenbow Archives/NA-4340-1

April 1909
Saskatchewan

Editor,

… If a man gets a woman that all she thinks of is silk dresses, paint and powder and soft hands, it's a bank she wants, not a farmer; and if she is too good to milk a cow or feed a pig should the man be gone, what good is she to a farmer? There are plenty of those kind of women in this country now. When a woman lets a cow go four days without milking because the man was not home to do it, as he was away threshing, if I had a woman like that there would be something doing when I got home.… Just a plain every day girl with lots of love and kind words and willing to work for her own good as well as mine is enough for me.…

Mr. Crank

July 1909
Manitoba

Editor,

… Now comes the hardest part, as it is a very difficult thing for a homely person to describe herself. Well I am 5 ft. 7 in. tall, dark brown hair, fair complexion when it is clean, but that's not often as it is covered with freckles, moles and whiskey-tackets, blue eyes, turned-up nose, large mouth and prominent teeth. Have exceptionally large hands and feet. Play the organ a wee bit and sing like a lark. I am very fond of riding and driving. Hate house work, but can at a pinch cook a potato and make a cup of tea or a cigarette (also smoke them, too). Now I will not say my age, as it will surely scare you if my description does not.…

Tomboy

October 1909
Ontario

Editor,

… I am fond of good reading, not merely for the pleasure I enjoy but for the benefit I derive from it.… I am a farmer's jolly young daughter, 5 ft. 4 in. tall, with brown hair and brown eyes and a clear complexion. I have never been told anything contrary so [I] guess I have always been considered good-looking. Of course good looks are always admired but without good qualities they don't suffice.… So I think we could better judge each other from what we are, and what we can do, rather than what we look like.…

Sunny Mayflower

April 1910
Moose Jaw, Saskatchewan

Sir,

… There would be nothing nicer, in my estimation, than to see a nice tidy house to come home to dinner in and afterwards for the wife to be dressed nice and tidy and a smiling face to come home to and chat with and talk over the affairs of the day when work and chores are finished. There are many little things [that] happen during the day on the homestead to make one a little cross and miserable with one's self and coming home and having to make the meals and wash dishes does not tend to make one more pleased with himself. But these small dark clouds are nearly always driven away by the cheerful face of a wife and a comfortable fire to come home to….

Weary Willie

May 1910
Manitoba

Sir,

… Being city girls we are very fond of balls, theatres, skating and boating, and our most enjoyable amusement is auto-ing. It is lovely to get up early, just as the sun rises and go spinning over the country for a couple of hours before breakfast. At present such pleasures are out of the question, but we spend most of our evenings at the skating rink and we are both considered good skaters and dearly love to watch a good fast game of hockey. In fact, we are very fond of amusement of any kind….

Merry Widow Twins

October 1910
Scobie, Ontario

Sir,

… To be a woman is … something more than to wear flounces, exhibit dry goods, sport jewellery, catch the gaze of men; something more than to be a belle. Put all these qualifications together and they do little towards making a true woman. Beauty and style are not the surest passports to womanhood…. A woman's worth is to be estimated by the real goodness of her heart, the greatness of her soul, and the purity of her character, and a woman with a kindly disposition and well balanced temper is both lovely and attractive be her face ever so plain and her figure ever so homely. She makes the best of wives and the truest of mothers. If the boys are savages we want the girls to tame them, but only a true and noble woman can….

Canadian Girl

June 1911
Hopewill Hill, New Brunswick

Sir,
May two New Brunswick lassies enter your charming circle and have their little say?... Siamese Twin No. 1 is a fascinating school ma'am of 20. Has brown hair and hypnotising hazel green eyes; not less than five and not over six feet tall; weight about 125 lbs. Neither smokes nor chews. Is an exquisite cook; can cook anything that you may mention, and can play the organ in moderation. Siamese Twin No. 2 is a captivating miss of 17 summers, with flashing brown eyes, a wealth of golden brown tresses, a peach bloom complexion, rose-bud lips, and weight 110 lbs. As to accomplishments, they are too numerous to mention. Perhaps her cooking ranks first; in fancy dishes such as boiled water she has no superiors and few equals. When it comes to singing, those who once hear her never forget her, and her playing on the piano is equally brilliant....

> *Siamese Twin No. 1*
> *Siamese Twin No. 2*

October 1911
Burdette, Alberta

Sir,
I am 21 years of age, fair, like to dance, roller skate, fond of hunting and sports, and am passionately fond of girls and music. I think they go together. Rag-time ranks among my favourites. I should like to correspond with "Ted," of High Bluff, Man., who wrote in December's issue. She is my style: airy, jolly, full of fun and fond of a good time....

> *The Rag-Time Kid*

April 1912
Saskatchewan

Dear Sir,
... It always amuses me to see the girls advertising themselves by weight in the same way as horses are sold. Supposing, for a change, they, instead of saying how many pounds they are, say how many dollars they are worth. It has been often said that the best way to reach a man's heart is through his stomach, but as sure a way is through a substantial pocket book. When a man marries, his wife ought to be a real partner, and it is no shame to the woman that she was able to help her husband financially.... Some of the girls say they are fond of skating, dancing, horseback riding, etc. Do they imagine a farmer wants to

marry a butterfly? Are none of them fond of housekeeping with its multifarious duties, such as washing, baking, churning, etc. We all admire a dainty pretty maid who delights in outdoor life and amusement, but we love a domesticated girl who is fond of her home, and who does not draw the distinctions between men's work and women's work. The farmer wants a wife to take a genuine interest in all that concerns the farm, and her husband's as well as her own prosperity....

Hamlet

May 1912
Lena, Manitoba

Dear Editor,
... I am a lover of nature. I love to watch the flowers, grain, etc., grow. I am also fond of sports of all kinds. Some of my favourite pastimes are shooting, skating, horseback riding, and best, but not least, dancing. I am crazy over a 'hop,' as I call it. I am passionately fond of music; can play the piano and organ, and am endeavouring to play on the violin.... I am a farmer's daughter who lives in southern Manitoba.... I am just sixteen.... Now, if any young men between the ages of 18 and 22 years care to write to a "candy kid," who does not mind card playing, smoking or dancing, but abhors chewing tobacco and the 'rag,' would care to write, they will find my address with our editor....

Flora Dora

August 1912
Ontario

Dear Editor,
... Last year I taught in a section where there were ten bachelors—bachelors from choice, I judge—for it was certainly not because there were none of the fair sex. Perhaps it is, as Hamlet writes, farmers do not want to marry butterflies or look upon women as an expensive luxury. As a teacher, I know that some of these ideas that you men have concerning women are not correct, for I have not only heard young men express their opinion that teachers could not keep house, but I have even had them sweep the floor of the school-house after I had swept it when we were clearing the school after an entertainment. I think most of us teachers are quite capable of sweeping or of even cooking, for most of us have been raised on a farm. For myself, I can say that I enjoy helping mother with the work on Saturday just as much as skating or dancing....

Little Louise

November 1912
Biggar, Saskatchewan

Dear Sir,
… A number of young ladies whose accomplishments consist of dancing, skating, and horse back riding, would be sadly disappointed if they were living on these western prairies. We bachelors are the pioneers here as yet, most of us living in shacks about 10 X 12. As for riding horse back, I venture to say, not one in twenty-five of us have a horse which could be urged to canter with a pole.… The prospects for skating this winter in the district are a little brighter.… Then the bachelors who are fortunate enough to possess skates will resurrect them from a miscellaneous pile of sacks, wrenches, rusty cooking utensils, hob-nailed boots, and sundry other things.… I would advise the young ladies to be school girls as long as possible, as life will produce enough joys and sorrows when they can no longer be avoided in later years. Your letters are only laughed at by the western boys. The majority of us are working hard to make homes on these prairies, and have not much time for these sports except in winter. The young ladies who are needed to help us build up this glorious west are those of quieter habits and a little older than 16 and 17 years.…

23, Skidoo

June 1913
Alberta

Dear Editor,
I would very much like to correct the wrong idea … 23, Skidoo … unintentionally gave our Eastern brothers and sisters of we young homesteaders.… We homestead boys and young men are mostly from good Eastern homes … and while some of our houses may be eight by ten … the majority are larger, and when we attend house warmings and dancing parties, we do not wear overalls or hob-nailed boots.… As for laughing at the letters of some of our Eastern sisters, who write of their accomplishments in music or amusements, their letters often give colour, and make pleasant an otherwise long evening. Of course, if they intend making a home on a homestead, they should be more than sixteen years old, and should understand household duties, but jolly girls, as well as good domestics, help to keep a young man cheerful and contented while building up a home in the great West. Again Ontario Girl tells us that a young lady who dances departs from the paths of modesty. I beg to ask why, as they all should, and nearly all do, go for the pleasure of listening to good music, and meeting one's friends in jolly good fellowship.…

A Homestead and Bachelor Boy

October 1913
Bassano, Alberta

Dear Editor,
I have long been a silent reader of your paper, but I must write now to give 'Hazel Eyes' a pat on the back for her opinions, and her courage in expressing them. In these days of "Women's Rights," "Hobbleskirts," and "Transparent Blouses," it is really refreshing to find a young lady who has the real womanly instinct. Girls nowadays want to start where their parents left off. Their young man must have a good home in the city, fully furnished; an automobile, or team and buggy, and everything else in up-to-date style. That he must be financially able to furnish her with one dress for each day, and two or three for Sundays, dances, picnics, etc., goes without saying. It matters not to the modern girl whether or not her 'beau' can pay for all the pleasures she demands, so long as she has joy-rides, dances, picture shows, etc. He is A1, no matter where the money comes from. I have been in this country seven years, and I find that the young ladies who are willing to help a young man make a home are indeed few and far between....

Lancastrian

January 1914
Manitoba

Dear Editor,
... We hear a great deal of late about the common vices of men.... But we hear very little about common sins in women.... Or have they any? Lets see. Now surely no one is narrow enough to put frizzing, powdering, painting, etc., down on the vice list; screaming at a mouse or some sharp squeak is of course only a dainty feminine distinction; eating chocolates by the pound and chewing gum will score off the tobacco habit from the men's card. Now here is something we all look down on and abhor—a flirting man, but what of the flirting woman? Why we simply wink and pass over her—unless she happens to rob us of a follower, then we make piece meal of her and often, I fancy, wish we wore her shoes—poor deluded creature. Flirting is to a woman just what drink is to a man—the more of it she gets the more she craves for.... The habit when contracted in youth becomes part of her, and only the sorest trials can uproot it.... Leave the men to their pipes, girls, and fight against this thing which leads where no pipe will lead....

Highland Jo [female]

March 1914
Winnipeg, Manitoba

Dear Editor,
... This month's [January 1914] page ... is exceptionally helpful and interesting. Highland Jo's word of warning is very fine, too. If girls only realized how perfectly ridiculous they look with painted faces,

In her modest and "proper" appearance, this young Calgary woman exemplifies the moral rectitude expected of women in the early 1900s. Glenbow Archives/NA-4354-1

rouged lips and pencilled eyebrows I feel sure they would never indulge in such nonsense. They attract a certain class of young man for a while, but when the time comes for him to choose a wife, he in most cases looks out for the home girl. Girls, it is up to us to raise the standard of womanhood. Men do want good women; they do not care a rap for those dressed-up creatures who think of nothing but theatres, music halls, dances, etc., and do not know the first thing about domestic duties.... I like to dress nicely myself, but strictly adhere to neatness. I also like to see a good play once in a while, but certainly can find something better to do than fly around here, there and everywhere every night in the week. There are letters to write, fancy work to do, reading, etc. In the summer I think there is nothing nicer than a good walk and chat.... In the winter ... there is tobogganing and skating....

Trixie

May 1914
Alberta

Dear Editor,
... I am an old-time rancher's daughter, and have lived on the plain nearly all my life.... I am a great lover of horses, and have a small bunch of my own. I am one that feels quite independent as I can saddle or harness my own horse, and I am not afraid to do any of the barn chores. For the past few years I have been riding and looking after stock. But don't think for one instant that I am not acquainted with house work. I am used to doing any part of house work. When I am lonely and have no work to do you will find me thumping on the piano and singing at the top of my voice. I also have no objections to dancing as I have spent many a pleasant hour in that manner myself. Now I should be very much pleased to hear from ... "Sod Buster," "Thirty-two," "Golden Ear Rancher," and "Rain Bow."

Prairie Echo

June 1914
Saskatchewan

Dear Editor,
... I notice the girls like to give their idea of an "Ideal Man." I think they ought rather to think about how to make an "Ideal Woman" out of themselves. An ideal woman must, of course, be healthy, but above all she must be of a cheerful and amiable disposition, always looking at the bright side of things. Nothing is so depressing to a man as to have

a gloomy, foreboding wife. A man likes above all to be in a cheerful atmosphere. Girls in general are apt to place too much importance on good looks. Knowing how to prepare a good meal is worth more than all the styles that ever came from Paris. You will find the best girls in their mother's kitchens. Steer clear of the girl who lets her mother do all the work. Wishing you all success,

Bismark

October 1914
Melville, Saskatchewan

Dear Sirs,
... Now, girls, you don't understand the men, not one of you. I have had enough experience with the opposite sex ... to "know the critters" fairly well.... In the first place, know this, that everything masculine from a bishop to a bartender will bite at yellow hair, no matter whether it's natural or—just peroxidized. Yes, they will all go crazy over that colour, and the sillier and shallower the owner, the better they will like her. Another thing, men declare with one voice that they want a girl that can cook. This is the biggest joke on record. I knew two sisters once, both equally good-looking, but the elder had the advantage—so I thought—over the younger because she was an A1 cook.... Well, of course, they both had young men friends but the younger sister had three to her sisters's one. Why? Search me! She couldn't boil a pot of water without burning it. The elder was dark, the younger fair.... Somehow I don't trust blondes. I leave them to be the playthings of the men. Men form their judgements of girls from the street-walking type.... You may stick at home all day and all year, darning socks, cooking, washing, etc., and your dressed-up sisters who parade the streets ogling the men will carry off the "prizes" every time. So, girls, don't take that old-fashioned fib about good cooks too much to heart. Men say they have no use for the girl who follows the fashions too devotedly. Another fib. A man is as proud as a peacock to be seen in the stylish girl's company, and if by any chance he has to escort a plainly dressed or a somewhat "shabby" girl he will take all the back streets and hike along the shadows of the buildings for fear he may be seen with her. Another point is this: Men like a girl best of all who has financial prospects. I doubt if even the yellow-haired lassie can win out in competition with the plain or even homely girl who is heiress to a good farm or a neat bank account.... And, oh! how the men hate brains in a woman. It is a positive brand on a woman to "know" things of any account—things other than silly chit-chat and petty gossip....

Freda

December 1914
Campbellville, Ontario

Dear Editor,
... In your October issue I noticed a letter from "Freda," which I think
is rather hard on us boys and men.... In the first place, "Freda" says she
is no "old maid." Well maybe not, but I'll bet a copper she will be. She
then goes on to say that men form their judgements from the street
walking type of girls, but I believe she is mistaken. Give me the girl that
can cook a good meal every time, and it doesn't make any difference
what colour her hair is either. Again, she says men are fond of the stylish girls. Another mistake. I would far rather be walking down the street
with a quiet sensibly dressed girl than one of these high-headed ones....

                                                            Jake Hayseed

December 1914
Alberta

Dear Editor,
... Now "Freda," I am going to scratch your eyes out, for I am one of
the despised "blondes." I wonder if I can change your mind on one or
two points. Do you not think you are judging all men by a rather
insignificant type? Now, I am neither wealthy, good-looking, nor yet a
plaything, but have a good many nice sensible boy friends and having
discussed the subject of "girls" and "matrimony," etc., with them will
give you their opinion. The average man likes a jolly, practical girl, who
can talk sense, take in a few wholesome pleasures—skating, etc.—and
who dresses stylishly—when the styles are not too outrageous—and is
at all times neat, ladylike and good mannered. I don't think "he" cares
whether she has money or not....

                                                                Blonde

January 1915

Dear Editor,
... My! but I think some of the letters are swell, for instance, in the
October number ... by "Freda".... Some people will say that it is not
true what she says. I know it is, and know, too, that all the dressier (or
I should say undressed) a girl is all the more admirers she will have.
There is one thing that seems strange to me and that is, this: why
should young girls with pretty pink and white complexions, naturally,
want to cover up their natural beauty with powder and paint, and then
pencil their already pretty eyelashes and brows, and then that isn't
enough but if the reigning fad is a mole or wart on the cheek or cheek

bones, why on one must go.... Some girls I have seen in towns must have quite a job to eat or drink, because when talking with one they dare not wet their lips and they look so stiff and unnatural while talking. The fish hook fad. I have had many laughs over the little fish-hook curls. I was told by a friend that knew a young girl who was all struck with the new kind of curls, and as she couldn't get them to lay down nicely enough, she took a little glue and glued them to her cheek, on each side, and every one in her home was exclaiming: "how prettily your curls lie, Marie!"

Alfred the Second

May 1915
Alberta

Dear Editor,
... I have noticed some letters in different magazines and papers of late dealing with the Canadian men. One *[WHM]* writer says Canadian men seem still to have a very old-fashioned idea of the uses of a wife. Others that Canadian men do not appreciate women. I think Canadian men do appreciate women, but they have high ideals of what an up-to-date woman should be.... Some of the readers seem to think we Canadians are looking for a slave. Not so. We are not looking for the good-looking street girl with the fancy dress and hat, with the false hair and paint who can't keep a job for a week. We want the girls from good homes with high ideals and ambitions, who can cook and take care of a house, who always look neat and clean, who are good to their mothers, sisters and brothers, who have a smile for their friends. You may depend they will suit their husbands....

Johnny Canuck

October 1915
Mere, Alberta

Dear Editor,
... Country girls do not appreciate fine manners in a man.... If you are polite to them, and offer assistance where it would be gentlemanly to do so, be prepared to be treated with a very cool and indifferent air, instead of a thank you, or a polite answer in the negative.... Many a picnic and social has been a failure where it might have gone off with a swing, just because the young ladies have made themselves objectionable. What is the cause of it? Is it because they think too much of self and dress—why, it is nothing else but dress they talk of; in that case we can't expect them to find time for nobler thoughts and refection. I like to see a girl smart and neat in her dress, but please let us have a

little more smartness in manners. Surely, they cost little enough.
Believe me, the manners would command more respect from your
friends than the excess of dress would....

Mere Bachelor

December 1915
Manitoba

Dear Editor,
I have just read, with a very great feeling of disgust, "Mere Bachelor's"
letter in the October number, and think that when he would so insult
... the country girls, his manner towards them must be the same. If so
he deserves to be treated coolly and without a great deal of respect.
But perhaps he has been in the habit of associating with only the lower
class of girls.... "Mere Bachelor" is evidently judging all of the girls by
those of his own acquaintance.... As for the country girls talking of
nothing but dress, I think that he has mistaken them for the city girls,
as it has become almost a proverb that the city girls are more guilty of
this than are the country girls.... I have lived on a farm all my life, but
as far as manners are concerned I would not take a back place with
any city girl....

Country Girl

February 1916
Saskatchewan

I ... have seen some very interesting letters in the correspondence
page. "Mere Bachelor" wrote a good one. Although all the young
ladies don't agree with him, I do. From my eight years attending
dances and socials in city and country, and my ten years' experience in
reading human nature, I find that one-fourth of our young people,
more so girls from the age of sixteen to twenty, are in the grip of "flir-
tation, vanity and foolishness." Saying nothing of "manners, powder,
paint and style" used by this class of people, I honestly think they are
trying to make themselves look like earthly angels. But I don't think
they will ever get the wings....

Single Handed [male]

April 1916

Dear Editor and Readers,
... I certainly am not ashamed of my father in his overalls.... For
myself I like nothing better than a good long horseback ride, on good
roads, in overalls and leggings. I think when I get dressed in men's

clothes I am just about "it." I have been seen by nearly all my friends and I don't think they think any the less of me. I am fond of all outdoor sports and it is much handier to ride in overalls than with skirts flying, I think. But, of course, everyone has their own opinion. I cannot skate very good. Neither can I dance, but intend to learn....

A Soldier's Admirer

November 1916

Dear Friends,
... I am nineteen, rather dark, tall, and am a great reader, play on the violin a little, and am going to have a career of some kind. I think it is nice for a girl to know how to earn her living....

Rebecca of Sunnybrook Farm

November 1916

Dear Editor,
... We are three city girls who live in the east, and have been reading the correspondence page.... We ... would like to get in touch with some of the young westerners. We are seventeen years of age, about five and one-half feet tall, and are considered rather good-looking. Our favourite pastimes are motoring, dancing, skating, canoeing, and knitting socks. At this time of the year we attend a number of corn roasts and marshmallow feeds, and certainly have heaps of fun. Leave it to us to have the great times.... If there are any young gentlemen who would care to correspond with us, we would be pleased to write to them.... Yours in suspense,

Three Bachelor Girls

December 1916
British Columbia

Dear Editor and Readers,
... I notice quite a few of the readers expressing their views on "the girl in overalls." Of course we all know that farm work is hard on frocks, that is, outside work. Nevertheless I think they would have to go some [distance] to catch this child in overalls. Some girls take a personal delight in trying to see how masculine they can be, whether it is necessary or not. If one could be wholly masculine, I think it would be nice, since so many of us girls would like to be soldiers, but otherwise I hate the pretence....

Valley Flower [female]

January 1918

Dear Editor and Readers,

... I was just wondering how many cowboys write to the *Western Home Monthly*. I wish I was a cowboy, but am afraid skirts would not look very good on a saddle. But never mind, I can ride horseback without a saddle. We have ladies' pony races at our fair and I have won three firsts. I have a horse to break in to ride now; she has never had a bit in her mouth, so I am going to have a jolly ride soon....

Flora

April 1918

Dear Editor,

... One thing this war is teaching us, that the Canadian men and women are noble and brave. The men are gone to fight for liberty and righteousness, the women are bravely keeping the home fires burning, and in every spare moment are knitting. Formerly on the streets of any city you would meet women with a dog under their arm, or led by a string. But now it is the knitting bag. But there are still occasionally to be seen the silly fashion crazy ones. But where you see one woman

While many men expressed a preference for refined and educated women in the prewar years, most considered "school ma'arms"—such as this one from Nesbit, Alberta—weak, dull, and unattractive. Glenbow Archives / NA-3976-35

mincing along on high heels and pointed toes, with bare neck and chest in the middle of winter, you see at least five sensibly clothed walking with a sure tread and an earnest look in the face, as though life meant something more than following the latest fashion these days....

Isabel

November 1918

Dear Editor,

... The farmerettes in overalls have a big place in my heart, and I am proud to see the way the Canadian girls are coming forward to help and do their bit in the great war. Great praise is coming to them all, I think. As for wearing overalls, I believe they are the proper dress for the girls if they are doing farm work. Some think it is not lady-like for a girl to be dressed in overalls, but remember it is not the dress that makes a lady....

Gunshot Bill [soldier]

June 1919

Dear Editor,

Giddap! Whoa! Haw! Gee! Hi Imp, pull that rein tighter, easy round the corner. There! well, here we are at last. Just dropped in for a few minutes from Idyle Wylde. We feel so cold and tired, wonder if we would be allowed to sit around your cheery fireside and have a little chat. You will wonder what on earth has come rushing into your peaceful family circle in such a flurry. So I guess we must explain our intrusion to gain permission to enter. Just imagine two happy-go-lucky ranch girls still in their teens enjoying life's ups and downs, always smiling to be in style. Probably some would describe it as a ten cent grin. We're especially fond of outdoor life, and all kinds of amuse-ment, (mischief, oh, wow!). What harm can be done in dancing? None at all! It's the harm people make out of it for themselves, as there is good and bad in almost everything, and as for overalls they are the pure whack for farm girls. We feel perfectly at home togged up in overalls or boy's clothes, romping around doing the various duties of farm life.... Hurrah for overalls! Our stay will have to be brief this time till we see what kind of an impression we make on the readers, and how many nice correspondents we gain. We will call again when these frisky colts get broken in to stand still a few minutes. Gidday! Away we go. So long, everybody.

Two Idyle Wylde Imps

December 1919

Dear Readers,

... Some time back there was some comment on the "Boys" marrying "Old Country [English] Girls." Most people ask, why?.... When one considers a good many of their lives were saved by their careful nursing, it seems rather natural that they should take a liking to them. Then again, the bright and cheerful countenance most Old Country girls wear, makes them very attractive.... They make themselves at home with everyone, and do not think that every boy they meet is wanting to marry them. Everyone admires good taste in attire, and may I say they are adept at it? As I saw it, most girls after dinner were washed and neatly dressed, their hair done in a pleasing manner and all ready for anything that might come along. Girls, all the boys admire you when dressed in a becoming way. I am sure there is nothing nicer than to see girls neat and tidy for the evening meal.... I will get into all kinds of "hot water" for expressing myself thus, but it is simply my opinion of what makes the girls "over there" attractive.

Tolerable [female]

December 1919

Dear Sir,

... My real reason for encroaching on your valuable time and space is to pass my opinion on a letter written by "Contented Bach".... Although I find the average Canadian girl to be jolly and a thorough little sportswoman, I'm afraid it must be admitted that our friend, Contented Bach [who criticized single Canadian women for being too reserved], is right to a great extent. While on this subject, I might say that another thing I've noticed, since coming back [from the war], is the way the girls are welcoming the English brides who are coming to this country.... Before the war I noticed that the average Canadian girl was just a little bit independent, and was not willing to come halfway. Now, in England (and I think that most of the boys who have been there will back me up in what I say), the average girl is altogether different in that respect. She is so much warmer hearted and loveable, and I am sure more sincere, that it is no wonder the boys were so attracted and made so many matches. Although I have the very greatest respect for the Canadian girls I know, to be perfectly candid, I must say that I prefer the English girl, and I think it is time the girls out here were thawing out a bit and giving the English brides a little better and more cordial reception... I hope you won't sum me up as being a crusty old bachelor or woman-hater.... I'm afraid I'm a little bit too much of a flirt to make a successful woman hater....

Ex-Sergeant

January 1920

Dear Editor,
... I'm "sweet sixteen" and a native of B.C.... I am at present taking a course in short-hand, typewriting, English literature, languages, etc., to prepare myself for the realization of my ambition, that of being a newspaper reporter. I am very fond of literary work and my teachers think I will qualify for such a position. I was very interested in Yankee Canuck's letter and he sounds as if there were 'pep' present in him.... Who is a swimming enthusiast among the readers?... I love it. Especially in the ocean on a stormy day when you have to swim some to keep above the big rollers. Do many shoot? I drive our car and my chum and I often go out with my dad in the early morning.... I also, like most girls, like dancing and skating. We have had quite a lot of skating on one of the lakes already....

Brown Eyes

February 1920

Dear Editor,
... I thought I might try and put in a word for the Canadian girls. Now, "Ex-Sergeant," have a heart. I'll admit that a good many Canadian girls are "frozen" as you say, but the majority of the good country girls, I think, are just as friendly as they know how to be, and I have noticed that in a good many cases the "frozen" girls are quite often the kind the fellows like. I've known a good, warm-hearted girl to be left to herself, while the one who has neither a warm heart nor brains has presents fairly rained on her. How do you account for that, "Ex-Sergeant"?... Cheer up, "Contented Bach" and "Ex-Sergeant," all girls are not "frozen" and trying to enjoy themselves at the expense of the fellows....

A Canadian Girl

May 1920

Dear Editor and Readers,
... I notice there has been some discussion this last while about the frivolous kind of girls who go with the boys for the good time they get only. Now I think some of our readers have been rather hard on these kinds of girls. Myself I think it is quite all right for a girl to go out with a boy for an evening, and have a good time, even if they don't ever intend to get married and I also think a great many will agree with me when I say a young fellow is a great deal better off with the company of a girl than with a bunch of his chums.... I like the free jolly girl who

can have a good time wherever she may be, and not the one who thinks she must not look at a boy unless she intends to marry him....

Happy-go-lucky [male]

July 1920

Dear Editor and Readers,
... I have only been out in the country since last April and just love the fresh air, horse-back riding, motoring and cycling. I have a pair of overalls and oh, boy, you should see me jump around in them. All you girls who are on farms should wear them. One feels so free with no skirts around them, especially after having come from the city and being used to wearing hobbles. I have a small camera and a photo was taken with my overalls on....

Hokus-Pokus

November 1920

Dear Editor and Readers,
... I live on a farm in Manitoba where I am home and am a real out-of-doors kid. I indulge in all kinds of sport such as dancing, skating, swimming, motoring, baseball, etc.... My occupation when indoors is reading and piano-playing.... Farmerettes, I agree with 'Hokus-Pokus' that there is no time to be lonely on the farm.... I also agree with her that girls should not be tied to their mothers' apron-string until they are "tied up" to the man they marry. I certainly like an evening with a boy friend....

Dardanella

May 1921

Dear Editor and Readers,
Here comes a city girl to gain a little corner in your jolly circle.... Oh, no, "Samanthy," we [city girls] are not all too taken up with pleasures to write, not me, at least, as I always find it a pleasure in making my pen go some, although I love car riding, music, and dancing. Oh, "Samanthy," you say you don't dance, skate nor anything. Why, you don't know what you are missing.... My ambition is to take up aviation. Perhaps you will think I am very fanatical, but just now I am taking up too much room and must bring my prosy letter to an abrupt conclusion. Will some of the readers write?...

Bashful 18

August 1922

Dear Editor and Readers,
… There is not any earthly reason why a girl should not discreetly use a little powder and paint to enhance her appearance and at the same time give her a valuable asset in life. It is ridiculous to insinuate that because a young lady powders slightly she omits to perform the usual daily ablution, as in nine cases out of ten she washes and massages twice per day. Personal appearance goes a long way in life, and it is always best to cultivate it, male or female, city or country inhabitant.…

Rover [male]

October 1922

Dear Editor and Readers,
… I should like to express my opinion in a few words regarding the use of paint and powder. I wonder how many boys would choose as their partner at a party, a girl who is guiltless of powdering or spending time improving her appearance? Likewise regarding boys, the most popular are the ones who are "fussed up," as it were, and have apparently given some time trying, and perhaps I should say succeeding, in enhancing their beauty. Taking it as a whole, I believe the boys are guilty, perhaps not to quite the same extent, as well as girls, of the "sin" of powdering.…

Onoway [female]

December 1922

Dear Editor and Readers,
… I quite agree with "Onoway" about the fussed ones being the most popular these days, and if you can't dance the latest way around here, you'll have to sit in a corner and be a wall flower. I am a cashier in the theatre here and get very lonely at times, for nearly all the girls from here are away working in the cities. It is just as "X" says, country life is too monotonous. Nothing ever happens here. One day is the same as the next. Like many writers I am very fond of reading and dancing. I would like to hear from some of the readers, especially some of the young and lonesome bachelors.…

Jazz Baby

February 1923

Dear Editor and Readers,
... I noticed in the last issue that "A Flapper" wanted to know if boys like girls with their hair bobbed. Why, of course they do. It improves their looks a hundred per cent. I agree with "A Flapper" when she speaks about people who think of nothing else but work from morning till night. I like to mix the work a little with play.... Now, I will close, and would like to hear from some Flappers about twenty.

Whiz Bang

April 1923

Dear Editor and Readers,
... "Mable," I quite agree with you. If any of the girl writers to this page engage in the art of sewing, they fail to mention it. Do not worry in the least about your letters not interesting us bachelors. I will wager that more than one read your letter with a feeling of thankfulness that the girl who can thread a needle and operate a sewing machine is not entirely extinct....

Crank [male]

June 1923

Dear Editor and Readers,
... We are what is termed "flappers," but we can sew, make all our own clothes, besides fancy-work and crocheting, keep house. We also read magazines and good books. There is nothing we like better than dancing and a good time, but we do not let that interfere with our other duties in any way, or our health either. We have weekly dances in our town, sometimes from eight to twelve, and sometimes nine to two. As a rule we attend them, as does everyone else in our town who dances.... Certainly it is alright to study and read literature, but what good is education if you stay at home and don't associate with others and let them know you are "alive"? We agree with "Yankee doodle boy" in regard to having a good time....

Punch and Judy

September 1923

Hello Everyone,
... I see where one boy thinks it is nice that a girl is able to do her own sewing. I agree with him, as nowadays most of the girls can only jazz. Well, I am not much for sewing, but I do love to cook. Cooking

and baking are my hobbies and the three years I have been married
have given me lots of practice.... Girls, they say that one way to a
man's heart is through his stomach. My hubby was a bachelor and my
little surprises are a great treat to him....

Hubby Sweetheart

[no date]
Dear Editor and Readers,

> I am a jolly Bluenose boy,
> I've travelled all the way,
> That I may join this popular page,
> And have a word to say,...
>
> I tell you all—I'm fond of sports,
> Be they indoors or out;
> I love a hill and speedy skis;
> Gee! you should hear me shout.
>
> Hurrah! for Georgie! Will you come?
> I have two pair of skis;
> Thanks, we will now descend the hills,
> And catch the winter breeze.
>
> I'd like to hear from jolly girls,
> Though they be dark or fair;
> It matters not their length of skirt,
> Nor if they have bobbed hair....

Barrie, 22

July 1924

Dear Editor and Readers,
... Readers, didn't the poem sent in by "A Jolly Bluenose Boy," namely "Barrie 22," just brighten you all up? "Barrie 22," I'd like to hear
from you, provided you'd care to hear from a girl. I like sports, too,
golf, tennis, but particularly riding. Please put on your breeches some-
body, saddle up that horse and let's go. Bet I'll beat you in the half-
mile. Hurry up, I'm ready....

Just a Western Girl

4 Courtship

*"What is courtship? Someone has said it
is composed or made up of sweet nothings.
Then let us have it, by all means."*
"Merry Sunshine" [1]

Courtship was another important stage in the romantic process, as this quote from a Saskatchewan correspondent suggests, and readers of the *Western Home Monthly* had a fair bit to say about it as well. At the time, courtship meant getting acquainted with a potential mate through a series of outings or get-togethers, followed eventually, if both parties agreed, by engagement and then marriage. For much of the nineteenth century the process involved a number of formal and public rituals, usually organized by elders, to initiate and allow for supervised courtship. But in rural areas and among the urban working class, courtship was often far more informal and unplanned. The rules became even more relaxed with the rise of large urban areas in the latter part of the century and the entry of women into the public domain, both of which made adult supervision and formal rituals less practical. [2] The purpose of this chapter is not to outline how courtship practices changed in the first two decades of the twentieth century, but we can infer the changes to some extent from the way people viewed the process during this period. The letters in the Correspondence column reveal Canadians' attitudes toward courtship in two ways—through the views expressed in the letters themselves and through the actions of the readers.

What, then, do the letters reveal? Most importantly, they show that correspondents strongly favoured the courtship process, as opposed to, say, pre-arranged marriages or little or no courtship at all before marriage. Most agreed that couples should know one another quite well before "tying the knot," as this would ensure a long and satisfying marriage. Thus we see many correspondents cautioning aspiring brides and grooms not to hurry into marriage. "Marry in haste, repent at leisure" was an oft-repeated phrase. When correspondents said they were "not in the matrimonial market" but simply wanted to meet someone—another common phrase—what they really meant was that they did not want to marry any time soon, but would still like to strike up a relationship that might eventually lead to marriage. The exact length of courtship was rarely specified, but it is clear that anything less than one year would have been considered too short. Waiting too long before proposing marriage, as in the case of poor Morganrodnaden, below, was just as inappropriate.[3]

The letters also reveal that a majority of writers approved of the unconventional method of courtship by correspondence. This is not surprising given the circumstances of the *WHM's* subscribers. Most, as noted in Chapter 1, lived in rural areas, where they had few opportunities to meet members of the opposite sex; "courtship opportunities" were limited to fairs and church socials in summer and skating parties or dances in winter. To the lonely bachelors of the West, preoccupied with their homesteads and faced with a scarcity of women in their region, the journal was the perfect way to "meet" a potential wife. As one British Columbia forestry worker put it, "the trouble with us bachelors is that we are out looking after our business most of the time and when we come to town we only stay from a week to a month and therefore don't get acquainted with the girls."[4] The peculiar circumstances that many westerners—both men and women—faced made it easy to overlook the traditional taboo against exchanging letters with "strangers."

Some writers even *preferred* courting by mail. Shyness seems to have been a common affliction among the bachelors and maids of the time, and courtship by mail relieved much of the usual anxiety, especially for men, who were expected to "make the first move." Correspondents who wanted to initiate courtship simply wrote to the editor to request letters from people whose own letters to the column had caught their eye, or they asked the editor to forward letters. In this way the editor performed the traditional function of "introducing" potential

A young couple enjoys a day on the water near Ogden, Alberta, 1918. Glenbow Archives/NA-2888-13

male suitors to women. Provided both parties were willing, correspondents then wrote directly to one another, taking the courtship process one step further. In short, the Correspondence column provided an easily accessible and relatively stress-free forum for meeting potential partners and getting to know them better. Most writers were grateful for this.

But while most correspondents heaped praise on the *WHM* for providing the opportunity to court through its pages, a significant minority favoured conventional courtship, in which men and women got to know each other face to face. Writers tended to be either strongly in favour of correspondence courtship or very much opposed to it, with the latter often accusing the men who wrote for partners of being lazy and cowardly, and the women of being unfeminine. The sceptics raised a number of objections, some of which appear in the letters below, but their main concern was that men and women who met through the column could not get to know each other well enough or fall in love and that, as a result, they would ultimately be unhappy as husband and wife. "It is like buying a pig in a sack," wrote one Saskatchewan male. "One would not know what he was getting."[5] Perhaps stung by such criticisms, a number of writers tried to conceal the romantic intentions of their letters, soliciting correspondents "just for fun" while simultaneously advertising their spousal attributes and soliciting mail from the opposite sex.

Supporters of the column's matchmaking, on the other hand, said that the sceptics' concerns were baseless. Couples were just as likely to fall in love by correspondence, noted an older man from Alberta, "as if they both had met in the drawing room and been introduced by that greatest of all hosts, the matchmaker, or had met sliding down the stairs just as we used to do years ago."[6] Some writers even argued that people could learn more about each other through correspondence than through personal contact. But even the proponents agreed that at some point before marriage was proposed, the couple had to meet; there was no open support for the notion of mail-order spouses.

In addition to favouring long courtships and personal proposals of marriage, writers to the *WHM* felt that it was the *man's* place to initiate any romantic liaison, by mail or otherwise. For women to make any advances—except perhaps with their eyes, as one woman observed—was considered improper. "I'm sure it is not the ladies' place to write first," asserted one Manitoba woman, "and she is not a lady who would."[7] That men were expected to take the initiative was perhaps best reflected in the proportion of men asking that letters be forwarded to certain women, instead of vice versa. Partial lists of these requests published in the magazine in 1907 and 1908 indicate that about 82 percent of the requests came from men.[8] Women who called on men to "write first" more often than not pleaded shyness as an excuse, but a fear of appearing immodest or unladylike was likely the main reason. Only in leap years—1908, 1912, and so on—was it considered legitimate for women to make the first move.[9] Even the simple act of soliciting male callers by correspondence— although not that different from the traditional upper-class woman's "coming out" or "debutante" ritual whereby daughters were officially placed on the "marriage market" at some social function—caused some anguish among women correspondents. This would account for the apologetic tone of some female letters and for the fact that several wrote to the *WHM* "on the sly," without their parents' knowledge. Few female correspondents were as bold as "Patsy and Cookie" or as coy as "Mermaid," below, in inviting male correspondents or offering themselves as companions.

Another attitude that came up frequently in the letters was the aversion to "flirting" during courtship. Flirting referred to single men and women who carried on romantic relations with more than one person, with no real matrimonial intentions, or who demonstrated romantic interest in more than one person. As the bitter letter from "Disconsolate" shows, flirting was particularly condemned in women because it implied—and could easily entail—sexual promiscuity. Writers did not usually make it clear why they considered flirting wrong, but they generally saw it as toying with a person's emotions, mainly by falsely raising their hopes and then dashing them. No doubt it was also considered disingenuous.

Attitudes toward courtship—and toward other romance-related issues—changed over time but not dramatically. Readers continued to favour long courtships in which men took the initiative, but they became more tolerant of what had formerly been deemed flirting, especially by young women. A brief debate, sparked by the sad letter in 1913 from "A Young Sufferer," took place in the column over the issue of how much autonomy parents should grant their teenage daughters in their relations with single men. The consensus was very much in favour of the daughter. As one male writer put it, "I certainly do think her parents are far too strict. Times are changing."[10] Evidently "A Young Sufferer" thought so too, for she defied her parents, secretly spending time with the men she wanted to be with.

The growing number of writers who expressed a desire to have fun with members of the opposite sex without a view to marriage shows the liberalization of attitudes toward courtship by the years 1910–19. Such hedonistic expressions were muted during the war—young patriotic Canadians were expected to think of sacrifice and duty, not heterosexual enjoyment for its own sake. But in the years prior to the war, and certainly afterwards, the *WHM's* correspondents gave ample evidence of their belief that heterosexual relations simply for the sake of having a good time were legitimate. Courtship, with its rules, rituals, and limited range of acceptable activities, was becoming the less formal process we now call dating.

This transition did not happen without opposition. The same writers who condemned the changing ideal of manhood and womanhood by the second decade of the twentieth century also bemoaned the flirtatiousness of women, especially "city girls," and the hedonism among young people. The extended debate about dancing—a portion of which is included below—illustrates the tensions produced by changing mores. Nor did the transition occur without

some confusion and anguish, especially for single women. We see this in the letters of "Farmer's Daughter" and "Contentment," two young women torn
between the old strictures against flirting and the emerging acceptance of the
more outgoing "jolly girl." By the 1920s this sort of ambivalence is far less evident. Young women, as well as young men, flaunted their heterosexual leisure
activities in their letters, especially their love of dancing. And fewer writers
moralized about flirting and other activities of youth.

Lastly, we turn to the question of how men and women writing to the
WHM differed in their views on courtship. As usual there was broad consensus
on the main points, with only slight differences in emphasis. Men favoured
courtship by mail more than women, in part because of their circumstances.
They were busy and isolated, and because the number of potential partners was
relatively low in the West, the Correspondence column offered them a greater
chance of meeting a partner. Men likely also favoured courtship by mail because
the onus was on them to initiate courtship, and this was easier to do by mail,
especially if one was bashful. The excerpt from "Dare Devil Jack"'s letter suggests another reason—correspondence by mail allowed men to avoid dealing
with their partner's potentially troublesome family, at least in the short run.

Some of these factors may also explain why men seem to have been more
liberal than women in their attitude toward courtship etiquette, in particular the
"rule" that it was the man's responsibility to write first. Their letters, especially
those from teenagers, are peppered with such phrases as "Don't be shy," "Now
Girls, don't be afraid to write," and "I would be pleased to hear from …." In
some instances, men even expected women to write first, and at least one suggested that women should ask men out on dates.[11] Nor did any man suggest
that it was immodest or unwomanly in some other way for women to solicit
male correspondents through a magazine, except where the woman was quite
young or appeared too eager to marry. Only women raised this objection.
"Another Scotch Lassie" wrote in 1907 how "amusing [it is] to hear so many
of the bachelors asking the girls to write first. On my own part, I would never
dream of writing first, and I am sure other respectable girls are of the same
opinion."[12] If anything, men were more likely to congratulate women for having, as one put it, "the courage to put their opinions in the column."[13]

The only other noticeable gender difference concerns the question of flirting. While most writers of both sexes condemned flirting in general, men tended to be more tolerant of male flirts than women were. How else can one
explain the unabashed admissions of quite a few men that they were flirts and
proud of it? The twenty-four-year-old Nova Scotia man who wrote that "I do
not either drink or use tobacco, but I certainly do like to flirt with the girls"
was typical.[14] What's more, when men did oppose flirting by their own sex, it
was often for purely practical reasons, namely—as the letter from "Onlooker"
reveals—that they could not afford to date more than one woman at a time.

LETTERS

April 1906
Medicine Hat, Alberta

Editor,
… Men want good wives and they will get them if they deserve them.
They must remember that 'no man e'er gained a happy life by chance
or yawned it into being with a wish.' A good wife is a prize and must
be won. One bachelor correspondent writes that he cannot spend the
time from the farm to look for a wife. Did he get his farm without
spending both time and money? Did he ever get anything worth having without spending time and money? How much more important
is the getting of a good wife?… It's their duty to get out and look for
them if wanted.…

A Western Young Woman

July 1906
Cumberland House

Editor,
… Your correspondence column seems to be supplying a long felt
want of the younger generation in outlying remote districts. How
many more or less forced marriages are brought through isolation
of young men and women whereas if they had had the opportunity of a wider choice, a greater resulting degree of happiness would
have been the consequence. Now, however, with the opportunities
which your magazine is offering through its columns, young people
may, though quite a distance apart, enter into a friendly correspondence with the ultimate view of finding a mate suitable in temperament, etc.…

Far North

October 1906
Rouleau

Editor,
… Courtship by correspondence is too much like a lottery game to
suit me. Might as well get married and try to keep house on the correspondence plan too. I believe that before making a final choice for
life, both parties should be able to meet one another in their everyday
home or business life and so get an idea of each other's real character.

If this were more often the case there would be less use for the old saying: "Marry in haste, repent at leisure."...

Jabez

November 1906
Saskatoon, Saskatchewan

Dear Editor,
... I think if the person that wrote that letter [denouncing courtship
by correspondence] would place himself in the same position that
some of us bachelors are in, they might look at the other side. Many

*As attitudes toward courtship relaxed, couples increasingly viewed the process—now called dat-
ing—as an end in itself. This couple from Calgary in the early 1900s were less likely to marry
one another than an earlier generation of courting couples. Glenbow Archives/NA-4910-8*

of us have very little chance to meet with young ladies, or any marriageable ladies. Now, if a correspondence can be started through your paper, Mr. Editor, I think it will be a big help for that will give both parties a chance to become acquainted; they will soon know whether they will make suitable partners in life for each other....

White Head

July 1907
Paynton, Saskatchewan

Editor,
I am of late a reader of your well known magazine ... and must say it is a boon to the single farmers, especially the correspondence column which is, I think, an excellent way for some of us bachelors that live a little bit out of the way to get acquainted with girls that want homes in the West. Some might call them [women] bold and forward, but for my part, I think they are brave and plucky....

Interested Westerner

August 1907
Calgary, Alberta

Editor,
Your correspondence column continues to grow in interest, and I hope so many deserving young men will get suitable partners. But they must take the advice of 'Black-eyed Susan' and let the correspondence continue for six months at least before thinking of matrimony. Then, with the assistance of some kindly disposed neighbour who might invited the young lady to spend a holiday, meetings could be brought about and perhaps result in a life partnership....

Aliquis

August 1907
Ontario

Editor,
... I think but few men would respect a girl who commenced a correspondence with them in the hope one would invite her to marry him. Let us have all the fun possible but let us not forget the dignity of Canadian womanhood in pursuing it....

Light O' the Morning [female]

September 1907
Ebor, Manitoba

Editor,

… A good many girls have a touch of this flirting disease and think they are smart, and many men the same. When they have cheated and deceived some poor wretch who has tried to do a square deal, they only giggle…. I myself am English, and am very proud of the fact, but I am sorry to have to admit that I have seen more flirting and deceit among English girls than among either Canadians or Americans; 50% of them will go anywhere and everywhere with every gawk that asks them, even when they are supposed to be engaged….

A Happy Clodhopper [male]

September 1907
Saskatchewan

Editor,

… There are the correspondence columns,… and who knows but the hope that is stirred in our hearts by receiving a nice, friendly letter from someone of the opposite sex may grow and ripen till at last we shall find ourselves cheerfully answering the questions the preacher puts to us that unite two willing hearts for better or worse. I think it a bad policy to be too hasty. One should take time and think of the matter—don't jump at conclusions; never take a life partner on correspondence only. Get acquainted, have at least a year's courtship, and then one should be able to decide one way or the other….

Merry Sunshine [male]

December 1907
Oak River, Manitoba

Editor,

… My friends call me handsome, but they also say, you go too fast. Well, girls, I will tell you how I acquired that habit. I was all struck on a very pretty girl once and the old man ordered me off the place. I went next week, I came back again. She told me he was away and would not be home until late. Well, girls, I bid her good night … when the old man came in and hoisted me out; he followed swiftly and I did not only trot down the road, I galloped…. I am taking this method [correspondence] of getting a pretty wife, for really, I think it safer….

Dare Devil Jack

January 1908
Alberta

Editor
... Now, while speaking of dancing, do any of our fair sex ever stop to consider how young men are badly hurt in feelings sometimes at the dance? We
engage them for a dance and when the time comes to go on the floor they
tell us they were [already] engaged [to dance] and go with someone else or
[say] they forgot. I have seen one girl play this game as often as ten times in
one evening. Now, this is the way it affects some young men: they go away
and get drunk to forget about it. If you have a brother, think how he would
like to be treated that way and then don't treat some other girl's brother in
that manner.... I believe a good deed is always appreciated even by our ene-
mies, but where does a bad one ever stop, especially if our fair sex plays one
on us?...

Rev. Dooley

May 1908
Saskatchewan

Editor,
... I was particularly interested in the February numbers as there were
so many letters from the fair sex of quite tender years. I expected they
would be at school at that age instead of asking boys of 20 or 21 to
correspond. I wonder if their parents know....

Lonely

June 1908
Glen Logan, Saskatchewan

Editor,
... I wonder if "Saskatchewan Beauty" really means what she says
about wanting to be married before Easter. I hope she is joking, for
I do not like to see anything unmaidenly in a girl and I think the
majority of the bachelors are with me in that. There is nothing we
adore quite as much as a womanly woman. I do not say that it is
not womanly to wish to be happily settled in a home of your own,
but I do maintain that the exhibition of undue haste or eagerness
is unmaidenly....

Quiz

September 1908
Saskatchewan

Editor,
... Why are the majority of "contributors" to the columns girls and young
ones? Can they find no sympathetic person in their own neighbourhood,

*Between 1905 and 1924, young Canadians strongly believed in the courtship process, whether
through correspondence or in person. This group from Rockyford, Alberta, is clearly enjoying
their sleigh ride together. Glenbow Archives/NA-3539-3*

or are they so lovesick? If the latter be the case, I do not know girls! And why do the boys and men advertise for wives? Have they not courage enough to speak what they would rather write? If so, they are unfit for even writing. If they cannot get a wife without writing for her, they are unworthy of one at all. How can we expect a girl to marry an unknown man of whom she knows nothing or what little she does know may only be from his letters, and we may be sure that they are elaborate, without arousing suspicion. Would a man do it? I doubt it. But many do it, but it is so small a percentage that it is hardly worth mentioning....

Dolly Dimple's Darling

November 1908
Saskatchewan

Editor,
... "Lalla Rookh" thinks it would not be ladylike for her to write first. I do not think it would be out of the way and I would like very much to hear from her and would answer promptly....

Cingalee

January 1909
Regina, Saskatchewan

Editor,
... Many of the writers claim that he or she does not believe in marriage by correspondence only or getting a life companion by the mail order plan. Now from the very nature of things, the parties involved must necessarily see each other before [a] marriage contract can be very well executed and they would be very foolish indeed if they did not verify the truth of the statements made during correspondence and find out something of the antecedents of each other beforehand. I believe an intelligent young man or woman can read character and disposition more intelligently from written language than from spoken language. A well written letter seems to be the unerring reflection of intelligence, character and disposition. If any shamming or misrepresentation is committed, it must be done by telling an untruth or lying in written form, which most people are reluctant to do, while on the other hand, in personal communication the one trying to make a favourable impression can perform all sorts of little pet shamming and false actions in order to hide her real disposition and character. I personally know a number of correspondence marriages in the Western States who live ordinarily happy together and some are exceedingly happy....

Teddie Bear

January 1909
Cambridge, Nova Scotia

Editor,

... I think "Shy Ann" must have a soft streak somewhere. In the first place she calls herself an old maid, and I think girls who call themselves by that name at seventeen years of age must be in a great hurry to get married. In the second place she writes "I want to be loved; I want to be loved, but I am so shy." She seems very shy for a girl of her age, does she not? She also writes she is not the one to land the boys. I should say she was right for once, for if there is anything we boys don't like it is a flirt....

A Nova Scotia Lad

April 1909
Calgary, Alberta

Editor,

... My object in writing is to get up a correspondence with some of the jolly, good-natured girls for pastime. I am strictly out of the matrimonial list. Intend taking a long chance and wait a few years. Now, girls, take your pen in hand and "get busy." Don't wait till tomorrow ... if you don't write now, I might die, or get married, or worse, and then you'll be sorry....

College Kid

June 1909
Manitoba

Editor,

... There is too much flirting nowadays. A great many of the girls will go with anyone who will give them a good time, as they call it, but in the end it turns out the other way. Young girls especially, who think they know it all, should be very careful in the companions they choose....

The Old Fellow

June 1909
Greenshields

Editor,

... I am ... of the opinion, young girls are too afraid of being old maids, therefore too hasty in saying they are matrimonially inclined. Young girls of sixteen, think carefully before concluding you are in the marriage docket, for after all, marriage is a lottery and "for ever and ever" is a very long time. Correspond with boys for friendship only, keeping your personal charms for your Prince Charming to see rather than read about. Let him first turn the tide from friendship to love, then don't be in a hurry, let the man come, "woo and win" his fair bride in her own house and neighbourhood. We can purchase any article with money by mail, but those bought with love have other forms than mail order. Pen, paper and stamps were never meant to do the finale in winning husband, wife, home, love, happiness and all....

A Young Wife and Mother

Local lakes and pools were popular destinations for young men and women eager to become better acquainted, or perhaps to meet someone new. Glenbow Archives/NA-2507-7

August 1909
Alberta

Editor,

… It seems that quite a number of the young men who write to these columns think the ladies should write first—at least they ask them to. I think that is wrong, unless the lady is in a great hurry to catch a husband, for some old maids might get in a sudden hurry and not want to wait for the bachelors to write first.… One wishing to know me further, I would advise them to write to me.…

For-get-me-quick [female]

October 1909
Craik, Saskatchewan

Editor,

… I consider that the idea entertained by most people "that it is wrong for young men and young women to correspond or keep company without serious views" is absurd. Which company would a young man profit most by? I should most emphatically say that a lady friend would be the more desirable, for a young man in such company would be training himself for self respect and gentlemanly conduct.…

Gandy [male]

January 1910
Ontario

Editor,

… I have the cutest blue eyes; you ought to see them. I'm training them now. They catch nearly every sweet-faced girl's eye. I intend to go to your wild and woolly West this next fall and would like to correspond with someone about the country before I go. If any of you girls with a sweet smile and coaxing look would like to write to a professional tease, you can get my address from the editor.… Who is that mischievous little honey-bunch that said she'd like to pack her slippers in my trunk? Trusting that this letter will miss the waste basket I will close, kindly asking you to forward the enclosed letter to "California Cowboy Girl."

A Fusser

May 1910
Lockhart, Alberta

Sir,

... No doubt there are lots of girls who think it is not quite right to correspond with fellows whom they know nothing about. Possibly not, although I think correspondence is a very pleasant pastime, especially through the winter. I am sure a boy who will go out west as a homemaker and braves the horrors of baching and lonesomeness is entitled to at least one correspondent to help make things cheerful....

Pinto

June 1910
Buchanan, Saskatchewan

Sir,

... I replied to a letter which appeared in the *W.H.M.* ... nearly a year ago. I got a reply and oh! she can certainly write a nice letter. We corresponded regularly for nine months. We exchanged photos. I asked her if she would come West with me and she didn't say she wouldn't. I naturally thought she would and was going after her but she wrote to say that I should not come on purpose to see her.... I, of course, did not stop for that but wrote some more. And finally she wrote last month to tell me that she promised one of the western bachelors from Alberta last July [before she began writing with this fellow] to marry him and was going out there in April for that purpose. Now, wouldn't that jar you? It certainly did me. Why didn't she tell me then? Is it a weakness of the sex that they like to give us poor mortals pain?...

Disconsolate

March 1911
Newfoundland

Sir,

Can you find room for the scribbling of a "Mermaid"? What was that? Did I hear you answer in the affirmative? I hope so. Well, this being a beautiful day, with a cloudless sky and not a breath of wind to ruffle the surface of the water, I have borrowed sepia from the cuttle fish, a pen from the pen fish, and made my way to a large kelp-covered rock, whereon I may pen a few lines to your excellent paper, which even a mermaid finds pleasure in reading...Could some of the Western bachelors call on me some evening? I should take pleasure in setting before them a dainty repast, the menu consisting of "jelly cake," made from delicious jelly fish; "rock buns," made from rocks found only in the depths of the ocean; "sponge cake," from my own sponge bed; "float-ing island," and other delicacies. Oh, dear! I hope you won't think my chat too long to print. As the seaweed is drying in my hair, and my scales are losing their lustre, I must now dive....

Mermaid

P.S.—My "cave number" will be with the editor. Matrimonially inclined? Oh, no! Who ever heard of a modest mermaid so inclined?—M.

October 1912
Irvine

Dear Editor,
... Well girls, as this [is] leap year I presume you are looking after all the likely looking young men in your respective neighbourhoods. It is really rather hard on the man who is a ladies' favourite, though, don't you think? You see, he can't very well accept more than one [invitation to go out], and if he has to buy many silk dresses, I am afraid he will have to be pretty economical for the next twelve-month. Maybe he will do like a friend of mine, who, when he had the question popped to him, answered, "Yes, but you will have to be the second."...

Onlooker

April 1913
Mount Forest, Ontario

Dear Editor,
... We ... are two high school girls, live on the same street, in the same town, go to the same skating rink, have the same boys to skate with, etc.... We certainly feel sorry for "Rover" who is going to try his hand at batching. If we two girls were only there we would lead him a live-ly time in his lonely home. We would very much like to hear from "Rover" and perhaps our correspondence would help to cheer his lonely life. Neither of us can claim the beauty of blue eyes, but we are told that our eyes sparkle with fun, and we,... enjoy a little dancing now and then, but not in a public hall. At this season of the year we greatly enjoy our skating, and would love to chaperon "Rover" down to our rink some evening, where we feel sure he would pass a pleas-ant and healthful outing. We would not like to tell our ages, as "Rover" might think us rather young....

Patsy and Cookie

July 1913
Ontario

Dear Editor,

... I am a young girl, twenty years of age. I have a good mother, but I believe she is far too strict.... I am never allowed to accept any invitations from any gentleman friend, no matter how good their character may be. I am never allowed to accept any invitations to a dance or to the theatre, if I do I must deceive my mother by telling her evil untruths—which I very much dislike to do. If I wish to meet any gentlemen it must be at some hour when "good people" should be asleep in their beds. Now don't you think it is hard on any moral young girl, who cannot enjoy enough freedom in her home, that she can bring a young man in to meet her parents honestly and openly, but have to meet him herself at an hour when her parents believe her asleep in her bed?—this is deceiving too. A young girl who is kept down tight, as the saying goes, will be like a bird locked in a cage and when released will fly on and on, happy in its freedom, until it comes to the end of its happiness.... Now, I do not blame all parents for their children's downfall, but I blame them for the start in many cases. Give a girl a little freedom in her home, let her choose a companion and she will not need to deceive her parents by slinking away like a thief to enjoy herself like other girls. Surely amusements cannot have brought all the fallen ones to their fate? Surely going to a theatre, or occasionally a dance cannot be the cause of many girls and men leading immoral lives! Our parents were all young once, but seem to forget it. Now, I love my parents and try to obey them. I do not deserve to be kept tight....

A Young Sufferer

September 1913
Winnipeg, Manitoba

A Reply to "A Young Sufferer"
... I should say your mother was to blame. The greatest error of which a parent can be guilty is of expecting to keep a girl innocent through ignorance. It has been proved ... that as soon as the severe restrictions can possibly be evaded, the natural tendency is to fly to the other extreme.... It is human nature. Parents must take into consideration the temperaments of their children.... These restrictions placed on the young can lead to only one thing, deception.... A youth has a right to expect the pleasure of that age. "Young Sufferer," you have but another year before you can act for yourself; possess what patience you can in the meantime, do nothing that would give people occasion to comment, then strike out for yourself, first making yourself proficient in

something. In the meantime I would suggest that you speak to your parents. Remind them that you are not a child, that you have certain rights, and that the rebellion which must necessarily arise from such repression, can but result in adverse action.... I can only in finishing say that "Young Sufferer's" parent or parents are to be strongly reprehended, and through ignorance and narrowness are driving this young lady into those deceits from which in their gross ignorance they are trying to protect her....

L. K. [male]

October 1913

Dear Editor,

... I am very much interested in the letter written by "A Young Sufferer".... I can heartily sympathize with the dear girl. Although I am only nineteen I have had some trouble in the same line. I have found out from experience that mother knows best.... There are so many girls who do not put full confidence in their mothers. Remember girls, she has been through many a rough path in life, and will do all in her power to save you from the same.... I think if parents are strict on what we girls deem as pleasures they must have good reasons. If you are not allowed to accept any invitations from gentlemen friends why not have a heart to heart talk with mother. Recall to memory her girlhood days. Whatever you do girls, do not make dates with gentlemen on street corners. I think our mother can judge our gentleman friends fairly well, but, listen girls, if you have a big brother he can "put you wise." I wish to say before closing, give your mother a chance, girls. She may seem a little old-fashioned in her ideas, but she has a heart of gold. She will prove a friend to you when all others fail....

Blondy

March 1914

Dear Editor,

... "Puzzled" mentions a case where there is a grown-up daughter old enough to marry. Young men come to the house. Nothing wrong in that. But it is wrong of the mother to talk of money and kill the germs of love in her daughter. True love is oftener found in the cottage than the mansion.... A little parental advice is sometimes all right to give our boys and girls, but, at the same time, I do not approve of interfering with their choice; it is often best to let them, as it were, weave their own web of life....

Jemima [female]

April 1914
Carstairs, Alberta

Dear Editor,
... I'll tell you girls, we got a raking over [by some correspondents in
WHM] for flirting. Now wasn't that terrible? Well I don't flirt. I just
have a very nice time. I meet lots of young men but don't care for every
Tom, Dick or Harry. I am very particular and if you don't believe me,
ask some of the boys. They all say, "stuck-up." Now that's not flirting....

Farmer's Daughter

June 1914
Saskatchewan

Dear Editor,
... As to a man or a girl who flirts, all I can say is, I do not want to make
their acquaintance. I have seen the terrible tragic effects of the affections being played with by heartless people. This Western land needs
earnest men and thinking women if it is to become truly great....

A London Lassie

July 1915

Dear Editor,
... People often tell me that men think it nothing to kiss a girl—
that flirting means nothing—saying that it is just a part of youth's
pastime and pleasure. I am afraid that too often these short times of
pleasure are followed unfortunately by a long period of disillusion-
ment of sorrow and pain. Why—if flirting means nothing, where
does the fun or pleasure come in? I would be delighted to have an
answer. To play with love's flowers, to abuse one's affections to pretend to love one just to have gifts such as jewels, theatres, boxes of
chocolates, excursions, etc. I merely say that the one who dares to
do this is throwing the black necklace in its own neck. How many
poor girls and boys weep on friendship's graves. Beware—
Beware—every dog has his day.... What is a flirt?... A flirt is a mis-
guided individual who treats all the girls the same and slams love's
door in their face.

Tob Bot

April 1916
Saskatchewan

Dear Editor,

… I am pleased to see some of the writers urging the readers to a higher life and aim than just talking frivolous nothings. Dear readers, life is all too short to be spent in just having a "good time." Some day the Death Angel will knock at the door and we will have to give an account of the deeds done in the body. Let us be up and doing while it is day, and may our lives be pure and holy, and may our aim be, not how many beaux we can have on the string, but how many we can win to a higher and better life.…

One Willing to Serve [female]

May 1916

Dear Editor,

… I am very bashful and that is the reason I come to you for advice. Here is my trouble in a nut shell. I am very much in love with a young lady with whom I've kept company for the past eleven years. During all those years I've tried time and again to muster sufficient courage to ask her to be my wife. Once I almost succeeded.… Now all the bashful readers of this page will surely sympathize with me. What I want to know is "What am I going to do?" Won't some of you experienced fellows help me out? I do not wish to remain single to the end of my days and from what I've heard M—— say, I'm sure she doesn't either.… Now, dear ladies, I am sorry I cannot ask any of you to write to me because you see M—— might get wind of it and my eleven years serving would be wasted.…

Morganrodnaden

July 1916
Cereal, Alberta

Dear Editor,

… Will you please give me space in your correspondence column to come to the aid of "Morganrodnaden," for I know if something is not done for him soon, his case will be hopeless. I truly feel sorry for a man who is so easily embarrassed; as for myself, I could propose to a girl I thought enough of, without batting an eye. Now, Mr. Morganrodnaden, there are eleven years gone and you have done nothing, except disappoint Miss M., and you at the age of twenty-nine can no longer be considered a chick, so get busy.… Again you might remind her occasionally that this is leap year.…

Straight to the Mark

July 1916
Edmonton, Alberta

... I would like to say to "Morganrodnaden" that I've a notion that his letter is "Make Believe." If not I'm sorrier for M. than for him and I hope she marries someone else and teaches him some sense....

Criss Cross [woman]

August 1916

Dear Editor
... I also wish to make a remark in connection with "Lonesome Ernie"'s letter [regarding how women should behave around men]. What are we girls to do? If we speak civilly to a man, or pretend to see him, he thinks he is sought after. If we do otherwise, we are called conceited. When you look at it that way, Ernie, you will see what we are up against....

Contentment

November 1916

Dear Editor and Members,
I did it! I asked M—— to marry me, and now won't you all congratulate me, my friends? I'm the happiest man alive. If I had only known it was so easy to ask such a hard question I would not have wasted eleven years of happiness by being so backward. I suppose you will all be interested to know that M—— and I are to be united before five years have passed.... Any poor fellow that ever gets into a state like mine and thinks my advice worth having, just write, and I will gladly assist you as well as I am able.

Morganrodnaden

August 1918
Alberta

Dear Editor,
I am living on the prairie in 'Sunny Alberta,' and life out here is rather lonely for some of us.... I think if the girls ask the boys to come and take them to picnics and dances, etc., there wouldn't be so many lonely girls and boys in the West, but they won't do that; they expect the boys to have all the "spunk." In my opinion, they will have to wait a long time for boys of my set to come around. Now, I must ring off. I am only a young boy.

Bashful Kid

September 1918

Dear Editor,

... I read a few letters from members on the subject of having dances in order to raise money for the Red Cross. I was and am still a lover of dancing, but I have stopped going to dances owing to this great war. When you go to a dance I think you are not showing much respect for the boys who have just paid that great sacrifice for you and me. If people over here lose a dear one they go into deep mourning for three months or more, but, still they can go and dance and forget all about the boys overseas. They may not be one of your family, but they are yours, and why not show a little respect for them....

Sky Scraper

October 1918

Dear Editor,

... "Bashful Kid" says that the girls should go and ask the boys to take them to dances, etc. I think that if the boys have not got the "spunk" to ask the girls, they don't deserve to have the girls....

Cutie Curls [female]

November 1918

Dear Editor and Readers,

... Well, Phyllis, I was reading your letter in the September issue and I do not agree with you.... You in Ontario seem to be so secluded when you speak of "Blushing to dance at a public place." Now, Phyllis, you just come West to where you have no picture shows or rinks, and you would be only too pleased to go to a dance in a public building. I do not believe in being so narrow minded. If you go to a dance it is not to say you have to associate with every Tom, Dick or Harry. A girl can keep herself a little reserved but not get too proud.... Please, Phyllis, put that notion of blushing to dance in public out of your head. There is no harm in dancing at all.... I have been in the West for five years and attend all dances and have seen nothing to kick at simply because I go there to enjoy myself not to look and find fault with others.... Please do not think I have no one in the trenches. Our family can count thirty on active service, and I do not spend all my time dancing, for I knit for the Red Cross and the Daughters of the Empire.... I also write to lonely boys and send them smokes and chocolate....

Kentish Hop [female]

March 1919

Dear Sir,
... Just a few words to "Marie." You advise "Phyllis" to pocket her
pride. I don't think it is pride. She may be more acquainted with danger than "Kandy Kid," if it [dancing] is carried too far.... I know what
I am talking about. Neither I nor my wife agree with dancing. We have
seen the great evils which have come from it. If dancing must be, let
the sexes dance separately....

Free Agent [male]

May 1919

Dear Editor,
I notice the members of this page are having a very exciting time tear-
ing each other to pieces.... "Free Agent"—I am glad I am not his wife.
I am afraid he and I would not pull very well, as I am very fond of dancing. I would like him to let us know where the harm comes in. Is it any
worse than skating? Not a bit of it. I can't understand why it is that so
many people grouch about dancing. He and his wife want to keep clear
of all kinds of sport if they wish to avoid all evil.... Let the young folks
discuss dancing, skating, hockey, baseball and all other such pastimes that
they enjoy....

A Boob McNutt [female]

July 1919

Dear Editor,
... Some of the girls and boys seem to oppose dancing. Well, for my
part, I cannot see any harm in it. I see that "Puzzled" thinks that there
is harm in dancing, because he does not care to dance while the
preacher is around. Well, I believe that true religion can be taken to
where there is dancing as well as to church. In fact, it should, because
I don't believe a decent young man would take his sister or sweetheart
to a dance if he thought there was any evil to come from it. If the
young people would conduct themselves like they should, I see no
more harm in dancing than playing a game of checkers....

Rancher

August 1919

Dear Editor and Friends,
... I notice there are several girls under the age of twenty years writing
to this page, and I think that girls under that age should be "cut out," as

they are not old enough to know their own mind, and think they should be more under the care of their mother, until they reach that age. Fancy young girls writing to the correspondence page, and asking that young bachelors should write to them. The mother of a girl who does so should give her a good spanking, and keep her more occupied learning what a young girl ought to know. Also teach her not to flirt with every boy she meets....

> *Not a Crank [male]*

November 1919

Dear Editor,
... Now, "Not a Crank," what is your idea about a young man marrying a girl of eighteen or nineteen? Should she get a spanking until she is twenty, or should she not be permitted to get married at all? I have witnessed several cases similar to the one above and see that the majority of them make splendid wives, where on the other hand a life of misery would have been led by the young man as well as by the girl....

> *Fly-by-Night [male]*

February 1920

Dear Editor,
... This is leap year. Why not have it that if the girls do the proposing that they also do the treating and take a nice box of cigars when they go to pay a visit? But, perhaps, there would not be so many theatres and joy rides then....

> *A Canadian Girl*

April 1923

Dear Editor and Readers,
I have been a reader of the Correspondence Page for several years, but until tonight, I have been unable to summon enough courage to attempt a letter. I owe my sudden inspiration to "Lonesome 28" who stated in his letter that he did not dance. I had become thoroughly convinced that every reader except myself liked most of all to "dance, skate, play cards, etc." I see that I am mistaken. While I do not condemn any of the above mentioned amusements entirely, I am greatly opposed to public dancing. You will at once ask, I suppose, why I do not oppose skating on a public rink, as well. This is why. The majority of the undesirable characters who usually compose at least fifty per cent of the attendance at a public dance, do not have enough wholesome courage and ambition to

don a pair of skates and expose themselves to the fresh air. They prefer
an atmosphere blue with cigarette smoke and modern slang, and often
actual cursing, well perfumed by the odour of "home brew"....

Crank [male]

August 1923

Dear Friends,
... My curiosity was aroused by one [letter] written by someone who
calls himself the "Crank." It is very seldom that one finds a young man
or woman who is so decidedly opposed to dancing as this party evidently is, that when I, being one of the "despised" who enjoy dancing
very much, read this, I was at once interested as well as amused.
However, I will admit that it was all very true what he said, at least in
many cases, and I am very glad to see that there are young men, even
now-a-days, who prefer clean company and sports to the lesser of
these, which one will find more often in a dance hall than anywhere
else. However, dancing is a mania with me somewhat, and I have not
met with any of the experiences mentioned, as yet, to any great extent,
and cannot see a very good reason why one should keep entirely away
from it....

A Steno

October 1923

Dear Editor and Readers,
... I do not see any harm in dancing in moderation. I am very fond of
it myself, learnt at home when I was a little girl. My parents did not
like me to go to public dances in the city when I was going to school,
but I do not see any harm in going to a dance when you do not carry
it to extremes. In fact I think it is a very enjoyable way of spending the
time. If you go to extremes, going too often, running outside to cool
off or not dressing warm enough, then it is harmful. I do not like to
see girls running off to dances two or three nights a week and then
coming to school or the office too tired to study or work. That is the
time it is overdone....

A Bookworm [female]

November 1923

Dear Editor and Readers,
... Yes, "A Farmerette," I most heartily agree with you. It seems as
though there are enough girls to go around, but it doesn't seem to
improve the lonesome conditions of the bachelors. Perhaps the old
bachelors are too bashful to pop the question? But now it will soon be

Leap Year again, and I hope all you girls will not let the glorious chance slip by. If he should refuse, he will at least have to get you a new silk dress. But never fear, I am sure all of us old bachelors would gladly accept, and give you two or three silk dresses also....

Launcelot

December 1923

Dear Members,
... I notice that dancing occupies a part in the discussions. For my part I believe in doing as you wish, at any rate do not make any dog in the manger affair of it. Just because you don't dance do not try to spoil the pleasure of others. This would be a sad world indeed, if all people thought alike.... It is possible to take harm out of anything. A meeting of the Sewing Club may spread more scandal and cause more trouble than a dozen dances. Every person has the right to attend to his or her own affairs, but not to meddle with others....

Huckleberry Finn

5   Physical Intimacy

No analysis of attitudes toward heterosexual romantic relationships, historical or not, would be complete without examining what people thought about physical intimacy. Unfortunately, the members of the *Western Home Monthly's* Correspondence column had relatively little to say about this, at least directly. Prior to the 1920s, and certainly before 1900, public discussion of sexual matters was considered improper, even immoral, not least because it was bound to inflame passions and lead to sexual excess, which in turn was considered physically and psychologically harmful. This was especially true for women, whose all-important moral purity was thought to be easily tarnished by sex talk.[1] In a way, then, the silence of the *WHM's* readers merely confirms one aspect of what is already known about that generation's view of sexual matters—that is, the less said the better.

Nevertheless, it is still possible to piece together from the letters in the column a rough picture of what Canadians thought about physical contact of a romantic nature. What sort of contact was considered acceptable prior to marriage? Part of the answer has been suggested in earlier chapters. Before World War One, for example, readers defined the "ideal man" as someone who exercised self-restraint with respect to certain physical indulgences, particularly alcohol; many readers also expected men to be "Christian" and "gentlemanly." The standards of moral virtue in the prewar years were even higher for the "ideal woman." One might assume from this—and from the puritanical mood of the prewar war years generally—that the virtuous adult was also someone who exercised *sexual* self-restraint.[2] This might explain the rather cryptic comment of one bachelor, who wrote, "I would like to get acquainted with a good Christian young lady with a view to matrimony in the near future. I am a total abstainer and am never naughty."[3] We might draw a similar conclusion from attitudes toward aspects of courtship. Members of both sexes expressed an aversion to flirting, with its strong overtones of physical, if not necessarily sexual, promiscuity. On the other hand, many readers condoned the display of affection between husband and wife as an important ingredient of a successful marriage, and such affection was not to be merely verbal.

The letters provide additional and more direct clues of the attitudes toward physical intimacy, and most of these weigh in on the side of prewar, premarital prudishness. But some letters, such as the one from a woman requesting a mate who was "tall, dark, strongly built and rather good looking" and "also very affectionate,"[4] indicate the opposite. Several women punctuated their self-descriptions with the phrase "never been kissed," implying, perhaps, that it was about time they *were* kissed.[5] One Saskatchewan bachelor emphasized that he was "not quite so near being an angel as some young men whose letters I have read" and wanted to marry a girl who was "not prudish."[6] Another ended his letter with the following quote: "For the girls they used to kiss me / Oh, I wish they would do it now!"[7] And an Alberta bachelor calling himself "Sunset Bill" (see letter below) argued that true love—as he had discovered from ample personal experience—was only realized through close physical contact with the opposite sex before marriage.

But of the thousands of letters sent to the *WHM's* Correspondence column during its nineteen-year history, these were the only ones that seemed to openly favour heterosexual physical contact—and quite tame at that—prior to marriage. Most letters that referred to the subject at all were far less open-minded. A number of readers quickly rebuked Sunset Bill—and men in general—for their "flirtatious" ideas and behaviour; the picture of the lecherous, opportunistic man-as-villain comes through clearly in several letters and is never denied. Some writers warned young women to be on guard against men like Sunset Bill, who would ruin a single woman's virtuous reputation by taking physical liberties with her, such as hugging, kissing, and "caressing." And at least one correspondent below, "Puzzled," spoke out against carnal desire as a motive for marrying. But direct references to physical intimacy in the letters are too few to allow for any generalizations, even tentative ones.[8] Were it not for the provocative letters from a Saskatchewan resident called "Josephus" on the supposed immorality of dancing, there would be no point in even attempting to determine attitudes on this score. The Josephus letters unleashed what became the longest-running and most intense discussion in the column's history. But more important are the insights that the debate provides into readers' attitudes toward premarital physical intimacy. Dancing, after all, involves a fair amount of direct physical contact between the sexes, or at least it did in those days. Therefore, how the correspondents felt about dancing—where it should occur, who should be involved, and what form it should take—also reveals their views on physical intimacy.

What, then, did the debate reveal? Most readers disagreed strongly with Josephus's contention that dancing was largely a public sexual act (invented by "lewd dancing masters," as he put it) and therefore immoral. Dancing was wildly popular at the time, especially in the West, where the opportunities for recreation were limited, and readers defended it as just that—a recreational pastime that was not only enjoyable, but physically healthy as well. Only under certain circumstances was the physical contact involved in dancing considered immoral

A romp in the hay with one's date would not have been condoned in the prudish atmosphere of the prewar years. Medicine Hat Archives/jws2655

or likely to lead to immorality. If, for example, the participants were motivated primarily by sexual desire—if a dancer harboured "impure" thoughts, in other words—this was deemed improper. Several writers pointed out that good Christians did not think about sex while dancing. In this respect, readers considered dancing no different from any other recreation for couples, such as skating—it was open to abuse by lecherous individuals but by itself was not immoral. Venue was also important. Dances held in private homes (known as "kitchen sweats"), clubs, or community buildings, where the guest list could be controlled, where people knew one another, and where no alcohol was served, would ensure proper physical contact between men and women. Above all, it would ensure that young women would not be seduced by "strange" men into doing immoral things, including "improper" physical contact, such as premarital sex. Most readers condemned public dancehalls in large urban areas for these reasons. Finally, many writers expressed the view that certain "modern" dances that involved close and prolonged contact—akin to hugging or "embracing"—were improper, regardless of the participants' motives or the venue.

If the letters on dancing are any indication, *WHM* readers believed that any physical intimacy of a romantic or sexual sort between unmarried men and women, at least in public, was unacceptable, especially between men and women who were not already well acquainted. The dancing debate does not reveal whether readers condoned *private* acts of physical intimacy between acquaintances. But given what we know about views toward flirting and physical self-indulgence, I suspect that good "Christian" men and women, single or otherwise, did not let their minds wander too far into the erotic realm at *any* time. The overall picture appears to be one of substantial pre-war prudishness.[9]

We know less about how attitudes changed over time because after 1915 readers of the *WHM* had next to nothing to say about the subject, not even in the context of dancing. We can only assume that the shifting standards of the ideal partner after 1910—from morally upright and self-abnegating to more fun-loving and adventurous—and the more liberal attitudes toward courtship brought a more relaxed view of physical contact before marriage.

What is more certain is that men and women did not differ much in their views of the question. Judging from the criticisms of Sunset Bill, women in the prewar period were perhaps more quick than men to condemn the man who took "physical liberties" with a woman. This fits with the finding in Chapter 4 that men were more tolerant of male flirts than women were, and with the fact that prostitution enjoyed a higher level of popularity among men—both urban and rural—than among women.[10] Aside from this, the sexes spoke with one, albeit restrained, voice on the issue of physical intimacy.

LETTERS

April 1907
Skafse, Alberta

Editor,

... I quite agree with one writer, who says, "the girls go to choir practice one night, to a dance the next night," whirling around there on the arm of some young man with a strong odour of tobacco and whisky perhaps in the room.... At those dances they meet with many young flip men who hug them in the dance, and strange to say, these young women never offer any serious objections to the hugging. No dignified young woman should permit such a thing; it may not be bad for their health, but certainly it is not good for their morals....

Happy Farmer

June 1908
Alberta

Editor,
I have read your correspondence column and am interested with the views of many writers. I wonder how many will find their theories upset after being married.... Life is not all sunshine; there are many little things to upset us and this is where trouble begins. Instead of fanning the spark into a blaze, let it die out and one cause to unhappiness is avoided. Often a tender, endearing word or caress will make everything run smoothly again. If you were lovers before marriage be so afterwards, too. It may seem foolish to some, but husband and wife can be far greater lovers than before marriage. It need not be made public but in the private of your home. Few men can ignore the thoughtful, ministering or tender caress of the wife if done with a loving spirit, or no true woman will refuse her husband's endearments and kindliness if done in the same spirit....

Experience

July 1911
Gull Lake, Saskatchewan

Dear Sir,
... It was perhaps a letter signed "A Happy Wife" in your April issue that almost compelled me to write.... I want to say that I take the opposite point of view to her in relations to "Hiawatha"'s letter.... I

This sort of physical contact—staged for an undated postcard—was frowned upon for unmarried men and women in the early 1900s, except if the couple was in an advanced stage of courtship. Medicine Hat Archives/jws2574

admire his heroic stand in respect to the world and the flesh, his fideli-
ty to his convictions, his discriminating task, when he with strong purpose writes: "I do not want to correspond with any girls who dance
and play cards."... I presume "A Happy Wife" thinks him narrow in
his views. But does she know that millions share his opinions? That the
best of our race condemn dancing, card-playing and gambling? That
almost a consensus of opinion adjudge these detrimental to the highest interests of man? Does she know that the line of morality and religion must be drawn somewhere and that there is a difference between
skating and dancing?...

Josephus

November 1911
Saskatchewan

Sir,
...When a group of young people get together and dance in their parents' houses or at the school, I see no harm in it. And if these same
young people sit down to a game of cards on a winter's evening I can't
see where the sin comes in. I am sure everybody will admit that some
city dance halls are not fit places for any young girls, and they will also
admit that gambling is not good for old or young. But, tell me,
Josephus, have you ever seen young girls who danced as I have
described dancing come to any harm through it, or have you ever seen
a young man who plays whist or any of the old card games come to
any harm by it? Many a girl drifts into bad ways, but if the cases were
analyzed, I think you would find, as I have found, that many influences
far removed from cards or dancing, had to do with her downfall....

Amicus Veritatis

January 1912

Dear Sir,
In reply to "A Prairie Visitor" of the October issue as to the difference
between a skating party and a dancing party, kindly permit me to say
that questions and objections have never been raised as to skating,
either in a party or alone, by ladies with gentlemen or otherwise.
Skating is a wholesome recreation and no charges of impropriety,
immodesty, or worldliness, can be laid against even the skating party....
With the modern dance, however, the reverse is the case. The fact that
it is questionable nearly condemns it, and instead of being a recreation,
is a physical, if not spiritual, dissipation, judging by appearances next
morning, and who would call it an accomplishment?... But the graver
objections are: That the attitudes assumed in the modern dances are

improper, to use no stronger word. Consider the attitude of the "rip-ple." The man places his hand upon the lady's waist, her left hand rests upon his right shoulder or arm; the man's left hand holds the woman's right hand as both their arms are extended, and in this position they circle through the room. At a fashionable dance nineteen couples were dancing the "ripple" and seventeen of the couples had their breasts lit-erally throbbing against each other. Custom cannot make an impro-priety proper. Would such an intimate and prolonged embrace be per-mitted in a promenade, or at a window to any Tom, Dick or Harry? Why then should such liberties be sanctioned in the dance? The objection is not in keeping time to music, or in the peculiar step, or in the dance itself, but in the liberty allowed and taken in the dance.... Another grave objection is that the popular round dances of the pres-ent day have been invented by lewd dancing masters and that the sex element, in an illegitimate way, is the spirit of the dance.... The chief of police of New York testifies that three-fourths of the abandoned girls of that city say they were led to ruin [fallen from virtue] by the dance.... The above are only a few reasons why the young people's society of any church should not give a dancing party instead of a skat-ing party....

Josephus

February 1912
Newfoundland

Dear Sir,

... I read a letter in the July number from Josephus, and I must say I think it a very sensible letter indeed. He expressed my sentiments so thoroughly.... Amicus Veritatis in the November issue writes con-cerning the same letter, but I think he (or she) is far too lenient toward dancing and card playing. Of course, we all know there is nothing sin-ful in the movements of the body and limbs when dancing, any more than in swimming or skipping, but in the company and associates it generally leads to, and the other vices that often accompany it....

Mermaid

March 1912
Bratton, Saskatchewan

Dear Sir,

... In answer to Josephus' writing in your January issue[,] I would sug-gest to Josephus that he is perhaps a little rash in the statements and conclusions he draws in his letter, and before I go any further I would say that it is the dance I am trying to defend, not the abuse of it.... The "embracing" referred to in dancing is no liberty.... After a young man and lady have gone through a dance, they say to their chums "That was a great dance," or, perhaps, vice versa; not, take note, "That was a great embrace," or otherwise. This, then, shows that it is the dance that occupies the mind and nothing else, and, therefore, there is no liberty taken; plus, to Josephus' view that "the illegitimate sex element necessarily enters into dancing." It does not, and Josephus can take the word of hundreds of husbands and brothers for it."... Dancing is a form of amusement enjoyed by all kinds of people: good, bad and indifferent, of both sexes.... [But] I do not agree with the public dance, because the doubtful ones can use the public dance to cover something else.... This does not apply to club dances or private dances, because club members form the big majority present in the one case, and in the other we know our host or hostess would not invite any doubtful characters. I am sorry that Josephus can see in dancing things which hundreds of Christian people never for a moment imagine....

Curly Bill

March 1912
Manitoba

Dear Editor,
... As a social amusement and a healthful exercise, dancing has much to recommend it;... By many it is unfavourably regarded in a moral point of view; but this seems a relic of that outburst of Puritanism that char-

Dancing was an extremely popular heterosexual activity in the early twentieth century, provided it took place in the proper setting, with minimal bodily contact and no lascivious intentions. Glenbow Archives/NA-4182-4

acterized the seventeenth century, and which saw sin in every joyous excitement. Dancing is doubtless liable to abuse, but not more so than most other forms of social intercourse. What liberty is taken in a dance that is not proper? In taking the position they do in the dance, they are not thinking of the impropriety or immodesty of it, but the pleasure they get. And how is dancing dangerous to morals, and in what way? If it was carried on in the form of a ballet, it might be dangerous, but as it is not, one has some trouble in finding where the fault lies....

Guizot

March 1912
Percival, Saskatchewan

Sir,
... Josephus gives a description of the attitude assumed by couples while dancing, and then goes on to ask if such an "embrace," as he terms it, would be permitted to any Tom, Dick or Harry. That mere question, sir, goes far to show how unfamiliar the writer must be with the conduct and etiquette of a dance or ball. Take first of all the position. The gentleman does not place his right arm round his partner's waist in order to embrace her, but to support her. Of course, I know perfectly well that occasionally one may observe two people endeavoring to squeeze themselves into the space that should be occupied by only one, but that isn't what I should call dancing. Neither does a lady at a dance permit herself to be "embraced" by any Tom, Dick or Harry. Etiquette orders and custom observes that before a gentleman introduces his friend to a lady, he must first ask the lady's permission to do so, and furthermore, the fact that the gentleman is willing to introduce his friend will assure the lady of the stranger's good character and reputation. I am afraid that ... Josephus has been singularly unfortunate in the dances that he has witnessed, or what seems to me more probable still, perhaps only heard of. Surely the fact that thousands upon thousands of good women and mothers permit and even encourage their daughters to go to dances does away with the stigma of impropriety and immodesty that your correspondent would try to have placed on what is our winter pursuits....

Phil

May 1912
Huronville, Saskatchewan

Dear Sir,
... Poor Josephus! His letter in that fateful column! I suppose, though, that it was too fantastically absurd to excite anything but commiseration

and pity. Why, Josephus, it is not an "embrace." It is perfectly natural that a man should so support his lady partner. And then he says "with their breasts literally throbbing against each other." My dear Josephus, allow me to assure you that this is not the proper attitude in dancing. The lady is rather to one side, is she not? She is not directly in front of her partner. Then, remember, Josephus, that nobody thinks of the attitude while dancing. If you ever danced you would know this. But there, everybody to his own opinion....

Debutante [male]

June 1912
Napinka, Manitoba

Dear Editor,

... I read Josephus's letter in the January issue, and as for what he says about dancing, I think he is very wrong, as I do not see any harm in it, and if it wasn't for a little dance once in a while through the winter I think that we would be all dead by spring.... I am very fond of all kinds of fun, especially dancing and card playing....

Honey Kid [female]

June 1912
British Columbia

Dear Editor,

... I was just going to congratulate Curly Bill on having such a normal mind, that he could dance and yet was sure there was no "illegitimate sex element" entering into the pleasure when reading a little further, I observed that he preferred the club or private dance for that very reason.... I would advise him to study the subject impartially and wisely, and he will be inclined to ... leave the club dance on the outside.... I have observed that even good people make mistakes of judgment and there are mothers who allow their daughters to attend dancing parties whose goodness is not to be impeached, but who ... have not realized what it might mean to a young susceptible nature.... I have been an observer where dancing was indulged in from 8 p.m. till 8 a.m.... A glass of wine, a bottle of whisky, keeps up the flagging footsteps, and adds the climax, that should make any mother pause before arraying her daughter in soft dreamy robes with bare arms and low neck, and sending her to waltz with a partner whose breath smells deliciously of—peppermint.... If there were more girls like Girlie who, though she likes to have a good time, demands innocent fun, the uplift to our Canadian home would be such as to give inspiration to the world....

Homebuilder

June 1912
Manitoba

Dear Editor,
... Josephus has a lot to learn before he can criticize dancing.... It would be a good idea for him to study the ball room etiquette.... He would also find out that the modern dances which he refers to are danced but very little. I think I can venture to say that there is not one person (who is a dancer) out of every five hundred in this country that dances the ripple. And, again, Mr. Josephus, I will give you another little pointer which you appear to be ignorant of, and that is a young lady does not have to dance with any Tom, Dick or Harry, as you seem to think they do. A young lady can pick her company at a dance, as well as she can at church, or any other social gathering. It is all right for people with evil minds and jealous feelings to bar such enjoyment, but on the other hand I think it is a good pastime and sport for the person who has a clear conscience and bright and noble career to put in the lonely winter months on the desolate prairie.... I myself have attended somewhere about twenty dances this winter, and I have never met one of those individuals that wanted to be hugged. I am proud to say that I, like all the rest of our prairie boys and girls, pick our company, and do not want to belong to the gyratory hugging society....

Sod Buster [male]

July 1912
Saskatchewan

Dear Editor,
... I agree with some of you young folks on that great subject, namely dancing. I don't think it is wrong for a young person to go to a good quiet dancing party in your own district where you are acquainted and spend the long evenings. I would rather go to a quiet dancing party than one of those ridiculous kissing parties....

Holly [female]

July 1912
Dundurn, Saskatchewan

Dear Editor,
... Now, I will take for my argument the dance that is not attended by the lower, vulgar classes where strong drink holds a prominent place, but the country dance, for instance. I, for one, would call it an accomplishment. It teaches us to be mannerly and courteous to those of the opposite sex. It gives a person an easy manner and a graceful

walk.... And since the attitude of the dancers are as they are, and the modern dance as Josephus terms it, cannot be performed in any other form, why should we question it?... Does it make any difference as to whether round dancing was invented by lewd dancing masters or by the Pope of Rome, since its intention of today is entirely different. Is dancing the only thing that leads girls to their downfall?... Take other games, such as spinning the platter, or forfeits, Blindman's Buff, or even skating. In skating you are allowed a certain embrace, and I have known skaters to take tumbles which were far from proper....

Kansas [male]

July 1912
Viscount, Saskatchewan

Dear Editor,
... Josephus, I think, is a little radical in his or her views on dancing. But there, we all know that dancing to excess is sin, so are many other entertainments and sports. This cannot be denied by anyone. I believe that even skating is sin, as I have seen many things occur in the rink that are just as absurd as those improprieties Josephus is setting forth in his argument against dancing. I am very fond of dancing, but you must know that it should not be over-practiced....

A Dancer [male]

October 1912
British Columbia

Dear Editor,
... I wish Josephus could live in our little wooden village for half a year.... Here the parents take their sons and daughters with them to the dances and all join in the fun and for a sort of a happy family. Now, Josephus, surely you do not believe that a father would teach his daughter anything that is evil? I dance with my father as much as with anyone, and enjoy it. Furthermore, do you suppose that, if dancing had anything to do with sex, girls would wish to dance together, while several gentlemen would be only too willing and eager to have the honour? If a girl finds dancing with a gentleman unpleasant she has the privilege of refusing to dance with him....

Little One [female]

The spread of automobiles—and the privacy they afforded young couples—combined with more liberalized attitudes toward courtship, no doubt made scenes such as this more common. Medicine Hat Archives/jws2565

November 1912
Ontario

Dear Editor,
... Josephus was criticised quite severely by some of the readers, but I enjoyed his letter very much.... Dancing is a great departure from maidenly modesty and is not sanctioned by the Bible—in particular, dancing in biblical times was never done for amusement, and never between men and women, or at night, except among sinful, worldly, and vain people.... The Bible nowhere sanctions such a thing as the modern dance. I know you all do not think just as I think on this subject, but time is short and passes quickly, therefore, do all you can to uplift and raise the moral standard of your fellow men....

Ontario Girl

December 1912
Mission City, British Columbia

Dear Editor,
... Now, I am a dancer and have been for some years, and for the life of me, I cannot see what harm there is in it. I live near a town of about a thousand inhabitants, and during the winter there is a great deal of dancing done, and if it was not for these dances I don't know how we would pass away the evenings. Of course, we do not dance every evening, but once or twice a week. Some critics of the dance object to the way a fellow takes hold of a girl in a dance. I admit that some dances don't look nice, such as the Turkey Trot, Grizzly Bear, Bunny Hug, etc., but out in the small towns these dances are very seldom seen. I cannot see any harm in the way a fellow holds his partner in a waltz or two-step, and I think.... "Charity thinketh no evil"....

Two-Stepper [male]

January 1914
Saskatchewan

Dear Editor and Readers,
... "Jane Craig"'s letter in the November issue has stirred up in me something that I have tried to forget. Why do parents let their sons and daughters blunder along in what they call love? Is it because they don't believe in love? Is there, or is there not, such a thing as love? I have often thought about it, and wondered why parents keep silent on this subject when they know that sometime sooner or later their children will marry. Yes, marry in ignorance, marry not because they hold love as something sacred and holy but because they want to satisfy their craving desires for things they do not understand. And there are parents who know these things, and still they allow them to go on....

Puzzled [male]

March 1914
Winnipeg

Dear Editor,
... Then about flirting. I think it is a great mistake for girls to allow caresses from men they do not intend to marry. What do they think of her afterwards? Why, they laugh up their sleeves, and discuss her amongst their friends. Every girl likes to be admired; it is in her nature, but let us live so that we shall be worthy of admiration....

Trixie [female]

August 1914
Coronation, Alberta

Dear Editor,

... To boys and girls of certain temperament, there is something strangely attractive, something almost sacred, in the attachments formed during school days, something in the "first love" which can never be experienced again.... But as a few swift years go by quite often one or the other forgets about the early attachment and marries and the other, perhaps it's the boy, keeps on dreaming of what "might have been." And so often many years are wasted taking a sad and melancholy pleasure in vain imaginations which might have been spent joyously in the love of other women. Then, after a time ... he finds as he holds some sweet girl close in his arms, that what he experiences now is love and what he has spent so long dreaming of was simply imagination.... Love as we are speaking of it here cannot be realized from an attitude of worship, but its full realization can only come from the contact of a close embrace.... And when a young man ... asks "Is there such a thing as love?" I can understand him and feel sorry that he has never yet experienced this sweet illusion. And when we say illusion we cover perhaps far more than half the cases, for what else is it when we have thought and dreamed since school days of something as more permanent than life itself and suddenly at twenty-five as you press a pure, sweet girl ... close to your heart, you find what you thought was love is not love at all and then e'er another year has passed this girl has passed from your life, her place to be taken by another. And so I say that when we characterize love as an illusion, as a sweet and passing fancy, we have come very near the truth in more than half the cases....

Sunset Bill

October 1914
Saskatchewan

Dear Editor,

... I think, "Sunset Bill," you are inclined to be a flirt, are you not? I suppose in your case, then, you regard marriage as a failure, since you can love anyone you take into your arms. Well, perhaps, I am mistaken, as I am but nineteen and haven't had your experience....

Conetta [female]

October 1914
Melville, Saskatchewan

Dear Sirs,
... I cannot help commenting on the letter of "Sunset Bill." It looks as though he were in the habit of hugging the girls all right, and he does not seem to care which girl it is, so long as it is a girl. It makes me "mad" to hear the female sex run down continually for the very faults which are so glaring in the male sex—flirting, fickleness and over-fondness for dress. Sunset Bill is a flirt, and also fickle, and if he isn't conceited, well—put me down for a bad guesser....

Freda [female]

December 1914
Saskatchewan

Dear Editor,
... Girls (you who are criticizing "Sunset Bill") I don't think you will be able to find one man in every five who would not try to hug and kiss a girl if he thinks she will let him. I believe in many cases they do it to test her, and I am sure his opinion of her is not raised if she allows him....

Brunette

January 1915
Manitoba

Dear Editor,
... Oh you "Sunset Bill"! I don't know what to think about you, but there's one thing I do know and that is I would not like to be the one you make your wife, for I would be afraid you would grow tired of me and be "holding some other sweet girl" in your close embrace, but I have had experience with those kind of chaps. The first chance they get, if they are not allowed to have their arm around the girl they happen to be with, they go off like a bomb. I've been over the road with all kinds of them, from the goody goody fellow, who didn't drink, chew, swear, tell lies or dance, right down to the one who does them all, and I found that the last mentioned was the one who seemed to have the most respect for me, and I always found him to be a gentleman in the best sense of the term....

Sammy

February 1915
Ingersoll, Ontario

Dear Editor,
… I have had the misfortune to lose my *[Western Home] Monthly* that
had "Sunset Bill"'s letter in. He seemed quite friendly with the girls
and I would like to hear from him and learn whether he has had any
experience with the "Rainbow kiss"….

MacTavish

March 1915
Capporn, Alberta

Dear Editor,
… Bravo, "Brunette," I just think the same as you say; if a girl allows a
young man to hug and kiss her I certainly don't think very much of her
and I believe all young men are the same if they would only be honest
about it. I should like to correspond with you if you will write first….

A Knocker [male]

April 1915
Saskatchewan

Dear Editor,
… I wonder how many lives "Sunset Bill" gave an uplift to a better life
or does he spend his time flirting? I wonder if he will know his ideal
when he meets her. I'll pity her unless she is like himself….

Britannia [female]

June 1919

Dear Editor,
… In reply to "Capt. G"'s inquiry, [I] would say that dancing has
played a very small part in the lives of the Canadian people during the
past four years. However, I do not agree with some of those modest
critics who would blush to "have a man put his arm around them." I
wonder if they ever shake hands with a man? If so, I am surprised at
their lack of modesty. The very idea of allowing a man to hold hands
with them!…

Soldier's Sister

6 Marriage

After identifying their ideal partner and courting that person, the next step for young couples whose quest had been successful (in their view) was usually marriage. Since this was a lifelong commitment at the time, it is important to ask how readers of the *Western Home Monthly* perceived marriage. Did couples eagerly anticipate it or merely accept it without enthusiasm as the normal outcome of male-female relations? Did they, perhaps, dread it? And how did readers see the roles and rights of husbands and wives? Did they prefer a strict division of household duties between spouses or a division of power and family resources that favoured one spouse over the other? Finally, what did the magazine's readers consider to be the ingredients of, or prerequisites for, a successful marriage? These are the main questions that arise from an analysis of the Correspondence column between 1905 and 1924, in addition to the usual questions, such as how views changed over time and whether such views were distinguishable on the basis of gender.[1]

The column's contributors expressed other marriage-related views, of course, such as the motives for marrying and the qualities they sought in a spouse, but earlier chapters have covered these issues. Chapters 1 to 3 suggest some of the reasons Canadians of this era sought to marry—loneliness, the desire for companionship, and (in the bachelor farmer's case particularly) economic security. Oddly, few writers mentioned the desire to start a family as a motive. Not so oddly—given the prudishness of the times—neither did they mention the desire for greater physical intimacy. Nevertheless, there is some overlap in this chapter with earlier chapters. The chapters on the "ideal" spouse address, in part, the question of what roles men and women saw themselves playing as husband and wife. Remember that the ideal woman in the early 1900s was one who was competent at housework, while the ideal man did not expect his wife to range beyond her domestic duties. The issue of spousal roles is explored more fully in the letters that follow.

The seriousness with which couples approached marriage—as a lifelong commitment—is clear in this 1918 wedding photo of John McGillis and Anne Hathaway of Calgary. Glenbow Archives/NA-4354-12

The letters reveal several things about how the *WHM's* readers perceived marriage. For the most part they favoured it. Several portrayed marriage as divinely ordained, as the "moral foundation" of society, or as an institution vital to the social good in general. But few readers tried to justify their support in this way. Most simply saw marriage as the normal and desirable evolution of male-female relations, particularly if one resided in a rural area (farming required large families at the time) as most Canadians did prior to 1920. Not that young Canadians had many options at the time. Living with someone out of wedlock was considered sinful, and remaining single was not regarded as much better. Those who were still not married by a certain age were viewed as almost deviants and saddled with the dreaded epithets "old maid" and "old bachelor," with all the unfavourable personal characteristics these terms implied. One fellow from Weyburn, Saskatchewan, reported that in his area, bachelors were called "dirty old bachelors" and faced intense pressure to marry. "Well I want to get changed [married] soon," he wrote, "so I will have the good opinion of the people."[2] Or they were the object of pity. One reader congratulated the magazine on "the good work which you have undertaken to introduce young couples who through no fault or failing of their own are doomed to the miserable single life."[3] The letter from "Idea" in this section indicates that women faced even more pressure to marry than men, which may explain why women placed themselves on the "marriage market" at a younger age and often called themselves "old maids" despite their youth.

The large volume of letters soliciting potential spouses confirms widespread support for marriage, but it would be wrong to say that the *WHM's* readers embraced the institution without reservation. Many bachelors, for example, worried that they would not be able to afford a wife. "The average young woman of the present day is a most expensive luxury," wrote one such bachelor from Edmonton. "Young men are afraid to marry because they are afraid they could not keep a wife in the style that most of them would like."[4] Women, too, had concerns. They worried that by marrying western bachelors they would become "slaves" on the farm; they were also warned, usually by other women, to think twice before marrying bachelor farmers of little means. A few correspondents even opposed marriage outright, either because they enjoyed being single or because they saw few redeeming qualities in the opposite sex.

Whether readers embraced marriage enthusiastically or not, most of them took matrimony very seriously. Marriage, after all, was for life. Divorce was not only considered shameful, but it was also difficult and expensive to obtain, requiring in most provinces the approval of Parliament.[5] It was important, therefore, that one chose the right partner, and this meant taking enough time to get to know a person. Better to remain single, said many writers, than to marry someone with whom one was not completely compatible. In short, no one should rush into marriage. "Let none of us be guilty of marrying merely because seemingly all our girl friends do," was a typical piece of advice, this from a precocious seventeen-year-old Manitoba girl. "Better [to] be denied the chance than be unequally yoked together."[6] The readers of the *WHM* may have been desperately lonely, or (in the case of bachelors farmers) in dire need of assistance, but this did not mean entering into marriage hurriedly or indiscriminately. Both male and female correspondents were adamant on this point.

If not rushing into marriage was an important prerequisite for a successful marriage—successful in the sense of happy and enduring—so were a number of other things mentioned by the magazine's readers. In order of most to least frequently cited, these included: the husband's willingness to provide his wife with a sufficient allowance; the frequent expression of love or affection toward one another (also known as treating each other to the "taffy stick"); the couple's willingness to compromise and tolerate each other's faults; mutual kindness and consideration, as during courtship; time spent together without the children; leisure time outside the home for the wife; mutual cheerfulness and optimism; honesty and openness; and a compatibility of interests and personalities. A number of writers also felt that marriages at a mature age, usually no less than twenty, were more successful. There was, in fact, no consensus on the recipe for a successful marriage. In some cases readers disagreed sharply, as over the question of whether granting women the right to vote would help or harm marriage or whether men should be financially well established before proposing marriage.

But an overwhelming majority of the writers did agree that there was one ingredient necessary—indeed vital—for a successful marriage: love. A couple in love could overcome almost any hardship, including poverty, but a loveless

Mr. and Mrs. John Speer of Calgary out for a buggy ride, c. 1908. Spending leisure time together away from the home was considered one of the ingredients of a successful marriage. Glenbow Archives / NA-4910-6

marriage was doomed to failure. Or so the thinking went. To some, love was the most important thing in the world. To the rest, it was only slightly less important. "Better a painful death in youth, or a lingering illness through a long life, than to live a hideous, loveless marriage" asserted one writer.[7] "Love is an absolute necessity to the happiness in a home," insisted another, for "where there is love, true, unflinching and everlasting, everything runs smooth at home."[8] Thinking, perhaps, that the burdens of marriage fell more heavily on the "gentler" sex, readers advised women in particular to marry only for love.[9] At least one writer, whose letter is reprinted below, even suggested that women become economically self-sufficient to ensure they married for love rather than for financial security. It was a radical notion at the time but another indication of how important love-based marriage was to the magazine's readers.[10] The exchange between "Skittles" and "Contented as a Bach," below, provides additional proof of this.[11]

The emphasis on love as a crucial ingredient of marriage is surprising in some ways. Given the scarcity of women in the West, the loneliness of many western bachelors, and the need for wives as helpmates in the difficult task of creating a homestead, one expects to find love being dismissed by the column's contributors—men especially—as a sort of luxury, a bourgeois sentiment reserved for couples in less dire straits. In fact, it was the very difficulty of western settlement that made love such an important ingredient in the eyes of the contributors. How else could a marriage survive under such trying circumstances? The overriding emphasis on love as a prerequisite also stemmed from the keen awareness of most correspondents that marriage was for life.

The only other marriage-related issues addressed in any detail in the Correspondence column concerned the household division of power, resources, and responsibilities. Readers were rather tight-lipped about the first two, but those who had an opinion generally favoured a "fair" allocation of power and money between spouses. Most readers assumed that the husband would be the main income earner and that he would provide his wife with an allowance to meet the household needs and her personal needs. The prevailing view seemed to be that wives were entitled to a fair share of the household income and should not need to find an independent source of income.

Most readers also felt that women should have a substantial, if not necessarily equal, voice in matters pertaining to the family, household finances, and the family business. Quite a few men said that couples should make financial decisions jointly, as a matter of prudence, that "two heads are better than one," as one fellow below put it. A few of the male writers, such as "Royal Arch Purple" and "Archibald," asserted the absolute right of husbands to rule the household and distribute money as they saw fit, but other readers, men included, rebuked or contradicted them. Perhaps western men could not afford to appear too authoritarian given their desperate desire for female companions.

The reasonably progressive attitude of *WHM* readers was also evident in their views toward the division of labour between husband and wife. The majority favoured a fairly traditional division, with women doing mostly household duties and men working outside the home. This is not surprising, for as we saw in Chapters 2 and 3, men sought partners with good housekeeping abilities and women wanted men who did not expect them to work outside the home. On the other hand, correspondents did not see these "separate spheres" as inviolable. Women were expected to help men with their work when necessary and vice versa. "I believe in each [partner] helping the other partner where possible" was an oft-repeated statement in the letters.[12] Readers viewed marriage as a partnership in which each spouse did what was necessary to build a successful home and business. Because marriage was expected to be based on love, crossing over into the other's sphere was also seen as a way of reaffirming or expressing such love. The letter from "Kallikrates," below, is a good illustration of this.

Readers of the *WHM*, therefore, strongly supported marriage; approached it as a long-term commitment; believed it must be rooted in love to be successful; and saw that it involved a traditional, but by no means strict, division of power, resources, and duties. For the most part, these views did not change during the period (although in this case the period ends in 1919, as virtually no opinions on marriage were offered thereafter). In particular, the strong belief in love-based marriages continued unabated. Only one change is noticeable. After about 1910, both sexes appear to question marriage as something attractive or positive. If the letters from (not so) "Bashful Bess" and "A Rose Bud" are any indication, women had less tolerance for the idea of surrendering their "single blessedness" in order to become financially dependent, obedient, overworked, and underpaid "slaves" of men; better to remain single was a more common piece of advice in these years. This greater assertiveness could be attributed to a number of things: the growing strength of the women's movement (especially in the West), the greater financial independence of women as they entered the workforce in larger numbers, their prominent role in the war effort, and the spirit of hedonism of these years, with its emphasis on unfettered leisure instead of matrimonial commitment.

Other signs in the letters written between 1910 and 1919 show that readers viewed marriage with more uncertainty than before. Beginning in 1913, for example, readers began debating the question, "Was marriage a failure?" The discussion, which went on for several years, revealed a fairly widespread belief that many marriages were unhappy ones but that they did not have to be. If young couples were not in such a hurry to get married, readers said, and if they took the time to get better acquainted—and, of course, fall in love—there would be far fewer failed marriages. One person even suggested that couples be prohibited by law from marrying before a certain age and without the necessary skills to make a marriage work.[13] The greater pessimism toward marriage is also evident in the sudden appearance of letters from young bachelors asking married couples what married life was like, and in another discussion, started in 1918 in response to the question, "Does love grow less after marriage?" The former elicited few replies, while the latter produced a decidedly mixed response. Perhaps the strain that World War One placed on many couples accounts for this less sanguine attitude toward marriage. But we can only speculate, for apart from the excellent letter from "A Soldier's Wife," the readers were unusually silent on this point. The increased pessimism more likely stemmed from rising rates of divorce and desertion and echoed the belief of an anxious Protestant middle class in the second decade of the twentieth century that marriage was an endangered institution.[14]

As to the question of male and female views toward marriage, the letters reveal some interesting differences. Women seemed more wary of marriage than men, which is clear from their frequent use of the phrase "I'm in no hurry to marry." Perhaps this circumspection was due to the fact that single female correspondents tended to be three years younger than male writers. More likely it stemmed from an awareness, fed by frequent warnings from married women like "An Unsatisfied Wife," that life in rural areas was no picnic. "After reading of experiences such as those of 'An Unsatisfied Wife,'" wrote one British Columbia "maiden of eighteen summers," "is it not enough to make one sit down and again contemplate 'single blessedness'"?[15]

Furthermore, male writers seemed more willing than females to breach the traditional division of labour between husband and wife. Far more men than women spoke in favour of husbands helping wives with the housework. And male writers were sympathetic to the plight of wives, noting that women had enough to do in the home without having to work outside it. They often suggested that husbands should help women with their work whenever possible. The comment from one bachelor farmer that "any good hubby would help his wife all he can" was typical.[16] One might argue that this progressive male attitude was merely a ploy by desperately lonely men to lure anxious single women to the West. But it is more likely that men did genuinely sympathize with the rural wife's lot, since they themselves, as struggling bachelor farmers, had had enough experience in keeping house to know how difficult it could be. "If anyone does know how to appreciate a good wife and home," wrote one Saskatchewan bachelor, "it is a man who has bached and homesteaded.... What does any other man know about the trials of a housekeeper?"[17] The 1913 letter from "Hank on the Homestead," below, offers a more detailed illustration and explanation of the western man's more progressive attitude toward gender roles.

LETTERS

June 1906
Crowfoot, Alberta

Editor,
… Cooking is something every young girl or woman should be able to do. But as for feeding calves, pigs, and milking cows, as well as weeding the garden, etc., why all this work is simply out of the question and I cannot understand how any young man starting in life would have the nerve to expect his young wife to do such drudgery. He should remember that a woman is not a horse. If I … get a wife I will never expect her to do as much as some of our Alberta bachelors expect a wife to do.

A Railroader

July 1906
Crossfield, Alberta

Editor,
… I don't believe in a wife being continually indoors working herself to death, but like to see her take part in outdoor sports, such as fishing, skating, hunting, etc. If I were married my wife could accompany me on my next bear hunt in the Rockies if she wished to go….

A Rocky Westerner

Men were more likely than women to favour a less strict division of household labour, perhaps because their own experience as bachelors had made them sympathetic to the plight of the average housewife. Glenbow Archives/NA-2674-3

July 1906

Editor,

... These old poke bachelors are stingy old critters and are protesting they do not drink or smoke, but I would judge that 90 per cent of them are not telling the truth. Don't believe what these old pokes say, and don't be too anxious to get married. You will simply be expected to help and slave to assist pull poke hubby out of a hole. Girls, remain single and make something of yourself in the world. Don't tie yourself up to some stingy old "Bach" to do his housework for him.... I am good looking, a piano player, a vocalist, and have a second-class teacher's certificate and am going on for my first-class. I am not thinking of such a thing as marriage.... We girls of Manitoba and the North-West should aim for a higher station in life than to get married to such old "toughs" as some of these are.... That writer from "Stoetzel" I hope will be disappointed. He wants a slave and not a wife. We are as independent as you, Mr. Bachelor. If ever I wed I mean to get a rich banker or merchant, etc. No mossback with hayseeds in his whiskers for me. Oh! No, thanks!

Youthful Manitoban

July 1906
Star, Alberta

Editor,

... I do not think it exactly fair of the bachelors to want girls to correspond, and have these girls come out to marry them, for suffer they surely will.... In many, many cases both husband and wife will have spoiled their lives, for they are assuming life's greatest duty without love. Love may come but to draw water, cut wood, rarely have a cent to spend, perhaps ... be six months in the home without seeing another woman's face requires, I should think, a deep and abiding love for the one we do it for. Think well, "Bachelors" and "Maids." Remember, a lifetime of joy or misery hangs in the issue.... The need, the crying need of our country is homes, but let them be homes founded upon right principles that we may not afterwards reap a harvest of woe.

Alphas [female?]

October 1906
Star City, Saskatchewan

Editor,
… A number of both sexes seems to me to be over anxious in wishing to marry.… Getting married is one of the easiest things in the
world, but getting a wife is quite another thing. I am a bachelor of 35
yet I do not despair. I think a man should be 75 before he is really
able to select a pearl of the first water in the form of a bride.
Marriageables of the gentler sex of today are as a rule a fickle and
brainless lot having nothing in their heads but marriage and dress.
Having hurriedly and blindly obtained both, they then have time to
take a common-sense view of the matter and in the majority of cases
find out their mistake and become flirters and backbiters and gos-
sipers—the most detestable of the human race. I hate a gossiping
woman more than the devil does holy water.… To my mind man
cannot know his bride too well beforehand. Afterwards, it is a little
late for character studying.…

Happy Jake

December 1906
Bankhead, Alberta

Editor,
… I think some of the writers have made a mistake in seeking a
wife and would do better to buy a machine.… How would the
bachelors feel, I wonder, if, after doing a good day's work over the
steaming wash-tub and house cleaning perhaps not getting the
last of the washing done until 7 p.m., they had to go out and milk
a few cows, feed calves, and pigs, split some wood and bring in
the water?… One bachelor says, of course, she could play the
piano in her spare time, go to town and mend the clothes.
Evidently he does not consider mending clothes work. He should
try mending clothes himself, as I did for some 12 years and always
found it very tiring.… I have done all the work mentioned, both
indoors and outdoors and I greatly prefer the outside work, as I
think the man has the best of it.… Remember a wife is a woman
and not a mule.…

Married Man

December 1906
Mortlach, Saskatchewan

Editor,
… I have not got the same idea as some bachelors have respecting a wife. I think that both husband and wife should be on an equal basis and neither a servant to the other.

Kalamazoo Boy

February 1907
Bugley, Saskatchewan

Editor,
… The question of matrimony is indeed a very serious one. It is something that should not be used merely as a matter of convenience, but should be the result of true love. My advice to the girls of Manitoba and the North-West is, never marry, unless that never-failing tie, true love, exists. Do not be ashamed of your choice even if he is a bachelor. There is no danger in marrying beneath you, if the union results from a love such as I have tried to describe.

Bachelor Chris

March 1907
Prince Albert, Saskatchewan

Editor,
… Marriage is too sacred a thing to trifle with. Men, as a rule, care too little for their wives and wives care too little for their husbands. The wife is looked upon as something to keep things right in the home but must look for no returns in the way of kind words and helpfulness from her lord and master…. Double harness [marriage] isn't the easiest thing to get along in. Little misunderstandings will come up and loving forbearance on both sides is needed to make things run smoothly. We cannot have too much love in the home life: I mean love expressed in words and deeds.…

Blue Bell No. 5 [female]

March 1907
Innisfail, Alberta

Editor,
… I have come to the conclusion that marriage and love is about all that keeps the world running. Of course it slips a cog now and then, but not often. That is just when the husband fails to have any wood

cut to cook dinner with, or the wife in her hurry, forgets to make the bed and the man retires first and so on. I say each one has a right to help the other. If the man works late in harvest time, the woman ought to milk the lazy cows, feed the pigs, etc. But on the other hand, the man, if through first, has a right to help wash the dishes, knead a batch of bread or sit up last and finish baking it....

Only One of the Many [male]

July 1907
Edison, Alberta

Editor,
... My house of six rooms is as clean and tidy as any in the settlement. I have every comfort, even a hot water bath. If I am sick, the lightest and most appeasing dainties are served to me. I can boast of clean table cloths, clean curtains, carpets on four floors.... If anyone calls to see me they are shown into my room—the room where I smoke and read, etc. No frightful noises emanating from a tortured harmonium [musical instrument] falls upon my ear, no family jangles, no baby's yells disturb the even tenor of my way—peace, perfect peace, and all for $17 a month! Oh, love sick ladies, curly headed, red headed, black headed, bald headed, home seeking homesteaders, how I pity you!... I want none of you! I have a helpmate who is worth a dozen of any of you. Your game is to take a fellow in.... Listen! My helpmate is an old sea cook I met in Montreal—a Chinaman!

An Old Sleuth

September 1907
Manitoba

Editor,
... As for girls, I know for a fact that there are a few real jewels—but mighty few. I don't want to offend the editor, but I have brothers and sisters, so I know what I am about to say. Readers, 75% of them [women] don't ever get their ideals. Marry for love, do they? Hooray! The chap that's the best looking with the most boodle gets the girl.... Now, I don't want any girl correspondents. I've seen and had enough of them to last a while. I would be pleased, however, should any young chaps from Saskatchewan, Alberta or Manitoba care to write telling me how prospects look out West.

Sly Si Sloam

October 1907
Alberta

Editor,

... Now I do not think that a woman should be made a slave of, nor do I think she should have all the say. If they [man and woman] marry for pure, holy love, they should work together for the best results. If the man is crowded by his work, his wife will not hesitate to help him by milking or feeding pigs and calves. On the other hand, if he has a slack time, he should return the compliment by turning the washer, or churning, or even helping her about her everyday work. But, above all, he should have a smile and a pleasant word for her. A woman appreciates that above all other things....

Happy Hooligan

January 1908
Saskatoon, Saskatchewan

Editor,

... A few words to sweet sixteens. Don't hurry to take up the cares and burdens meant for older shoulders; enjoy your girlhood, the care-free, happiest period of your lives—sixteen to twenty-two. You will be plenty young enough then; your judgement will be better then. The ideals of sixteen may not be the ideals of twenty and you will be less liable to make mistakes. I have been in love a few times myself—and hope to be once more. The first love is not necessarily the last, no matter how wonderful it may be, nor "nobody every loved so before." The

Correspondents considered love the most important prerequisite for a happy and lasting marriage, particularly in view of the difficulties newlyweds faced on the unforgiving western frontier. Glenbow Archives/NA-4179-20

bud of sixteen, just starting to blossom into womanhood, care-free, happy, smiling in sunshine and storm, is the most beautiful thing in all creation. Don't hurry to be a full blown flower....

Interested [older male]

April 1908

Editor,

... I am a young girl 21 years old.... I can cook and am a good housekeeper. I can cook enough for any white man. I can milk a cow or harness a horse, feed pigs and calves if they do not kick too hard. I like raising chickens and I can ride horse-back or drive.... I like dancing and could teach him [her future husband] if he is not too stupid. I would like a man that would let me go out when I like whether my work was done or not. When I get married I expect to be boss of myself. I do not want to boss my husband or his parents, or him to be boss of me. I do not mind feeding pigs and other animals once in a great while when he is away but I expect to go out with him sometimes....

Ellen Jane

June 1908
Petrel, Manitoba

Editor,

... It is no good of people marrying, in my humble opinion, unless they have a mutual regard and if such be the case, "hubby" will not object to getting his own dinner or supper once in a while when his "better half" is away to a ladies' aid meeting or other occasion and his "dear girlie" will not mind feeding the pigs and milking the cows when hubby is working late loading a car, etc. In other words, there will be no "won't do this or that" or "don't have to," for the aim of each will be mutual help....

Kallikrates [male]

February 1909
Manitoba

Editor,

... Now, girls, I think most of you are not so hard hearted that if you married a man you really loved (for when I marry I will marry for love) you would turn in and help him out a little, such as milk the cow or put in a little hay to the horses if he were late coming home from work. There would not be much work about it if you would help him a little. For my part I would not let a woman do chores, only in case of an emergency. I have a fair knowledge of batching and know something of what a good housekeeper has to do and would not hesitate to help in the house any time that I am not too busy, such as on a stormy day. I have been told that I am an expert dishwasher and a good cook. I have even put up a good dinner for the minister....

Total Abstainer

March 1909
Nutana, Saskatchewan

Editor,
... I notice some of the girls object to doing outside chores. I do not agree with them on that subject. Any girl who spends all her time indoors is generally cross and will not take a joke.... It is well to mix the work on both sides. A man should also do his share of house work. To even things up a wife should be a helpmate for her husband and he a helpmate for her....

Canterbury Bell [female]

July 1909
Meridian, Saskatchewan

Editor,
... A person is better living in single blessedness than to be bound to a person whom you cannot love and honour. Where love reigns supreme in a home it is next to heaven. I for my part am willing to do my duty providing my life partner does her duty. I would not expect to make a slave of my wife in any form and would not be made a slave by my wife or any other woman, or person or persons. I am a lover of freedom and like to see others enjoy the same.... You see, when I double up I am to be the head of the family or there would likely be a little fun if you attempt to govern or manage me. Or, as some people say, I am to be the boss. But I am not a hard or overbearing boss by any means for I am a lover of peace though when I rule I am firm always, keeping as my motto "Justice" to the letter....

Royal Arch Purple

October 1909

Editor,
... I would never ask a woman to work outside [the house], for I think she would have enough to do inside. I would only help her. But I can tell bachelors or any other men that a house is miserable without a decent,

respectable woman. Before I came to this country I used to say that women had not much to do. That was when I had nothing to do inside doors. Well, friends, I took up a homestead and lived on it all last fall and I would give anything to a woman to be working inside in my place....

Scotland Yet

December 1909

Sir,

... I would say this corresponding is alright for friendship and to help pass the time, but to be in earnest I would say take the advice of a lonely woman who is married. These men who write can say anything on paper but when it comes right down to it, keeping house on a homestead is not always the good apple on the tree.... We are poor, and I have to do any kind of work, feed pigs, hens, milk cows, help to make hay and feed calves, and that is not all, chop wood and make my own fires and so on. I can't sit down to the piano for we have none. It is mostly work all day and when I ask anything from my husband, he is generally too busy to afford me going away with a horse. No time to waste for a woman's amusements. If I want any money I have to earn it myself, and I have often gone to my father's home to earn it. Some men have the heart of a stone. They never stop to think about how they ought to treat women. They will treat outsiders better than their own wife, and I am a good cook and know how to economize, do my own sewing, make butter and have a garden. I do everything to get along for a poor farmer, but I get no reward, no thanks, not even in his heart.... I am sensitive and feel it keenly. Now it is too late. I dress very plainly and do not spend any more than $5 a year, if that, and that out of my own earnings. Now, girls, I hope that I have not led you to believe that most men are ignorant of the fact that they have a good wife and don't know how to treat her. Stop to consider the grave situation that may be before you. Correspond for friendship and company, but that is all. What you want to look for is good, kind, generous, helpful, self-respecting men. I think there are some fine young men in the West, who, when they had a good sensible woman would know how to treat her, that she would not grow stale in her love for him.

An Unsatisfied Wife

January 1910
Viscount, Saskatchewan

Editor,

... I would like to say a little about "Royal Arch Purple"'s letter.... You say you'll be boss. Did it ever occur to you that there may be some one in this country just a little bit more gifted with common sense than you are? Put yourself in your wife's place and see if you wouldn't like to have a little bit of say. You see, Mr. "Purple," if you start that game, your wife's ideas ... never come into action and she will soon lose all interest in your farm, your self and her surroundings and just eke out a miserable sort of life that is no more or less than existence. Now, let me tell you if there is a boss needed between husband and wife there's "bound to be a row." Surely the old saying "two heads are better than one" still holds true. And besides, my religious friend, your wife, you must remember, is one of God's creatures as much as you are and has a perfect right to have some say as to how her life is to be run....

The Dougal Crater [male]

April 1910
Lethbridge, Alberta

Sir,

I have been reading the *Western Home Monthly* with great interest ... and now ask your help in finding me a wife.... Of course, I would expect my wife to take care of the chickens, feed the hogs and milk the cows. Let me say here that chicken money ought to keep us in groceries and coal and also what spending money I might need. I would handle the purse. What does a woman need of money? Her place is in the kitchen. I can buy the one or two kitchen dresses she will need during the year. That is enough for any woman. If she does

The solemn faces of this 1913 wedding party from Coleman, Alberta, might betray the reservations many young people were beginning to have about marriage by the war years. Glenbow Archives/NA-4279-5

well with the chickens I might get her a good dress providing she can make it herself. When I come from town at night she must meet me with a smile and a steaming hot supper. I will expect all the chores done, of course. Now, if any young lady of this description cares to write to me, my address will be with the Editor.

Archibald

June 1910
Morris, Manitoba

Sir,

I have been a constant reader of the *Western Home Monthly* for a year or so and find the letters in the correspondence very interesting, especially the letter signed "Archibald" in the April number.... You just bet I can cook, and would always have hot meals ready for him, providing I had plenty of red pepper and fuel, but of course the chicken money would keep us in those necessaries. I'm just a whirlwind at raising chickens, and being of Irish descent I just love pigs. Of course he would handle the purse. Why not? A woman would only lose the money anyway. A husband of such unbounded generosity as to provide two kitchen dresses and a possible good one all in one year must be a catch. He surely won't want for a wife long. But I would not be as extravagant as that. I'm sure I could do with one by patching it occasionally and dyeing it when the colours wore out, providing he would lend me a pair of overalls to wear when milking the cows and feeding the pigs. As for the smile when he comes home from town, why that's easy. I just naturally smile all the time, and of course the chores would always be done. What poor tired man with his nice clothes on would want to go out and do chores after being to town? Hoping my list of accomplishments will meet with Archibald's approval, I look hopefully into the future.

Batty O'Toole

August 1910
Moose Jaw, Saskatchewan

Sir,

... [A] much discussed question today is the wife's share of income. Now, I think that when any man thinks enough of any woman to make her his wife he should at the same time make her his confidant in all matters pertaining either to the home or to his business, and he will be surprised at the help she will be able to give him.... Secrets between the husband and wife always were and always will be a source of continual annoyance and domestic unhappiness.

Every man should have the same respect and admiration for his wife that the darky had who, after his wedding, asked the parson what he owed him for his services, and when that gentleman replied, "Just pay me whatever it is worth to you, Sam," the darky said, "If I was to do that, suh, I is surely done broke for life." I sincerely believe that the fairer sex have the "harder row to hoe" through this life, and it is up to us who call ourselves men and who are fortunate enough to possess that greatest of blessings, a home and loving wife, to do everything in our power to make her married life a happy one.... I will conclude with this toast: "Here's to our sweethearts, may they be our wives; and here's to our wives, may they always be our sweethearts"....

A Former Michigan Boy

August 1910

Sir,

... I was greatly interested in "All Alone"'s letter of May. I wonder if he thinks marriage is the only thing that will make a girl sensible and broad-minded. I am not married, and am not writing with the object of finding a husband. Perhaps I think I am sensible enough, or again, perhaps I think myself too sensible to get married. I am a wage-earner, making a comfortable living and enjoy my work very much, and therefore will never marry in order to have a home. May I say that I think the biggest mistake parents can make is bringing up their daughters without any means of supporting themselves if it becomes necessary, thus forcing them into unhappy marriages. Making girls independent does not make them despise marriage, but enables them to see it in its true light. Such girls will marry, not at the first opportunity, but when they see a man they can honour above all others. "Girls, don't marry the first man that you think you could live with, but marry the man you don't think you can live without"....

A Mountain Girl

August 1910

Sir,

... I came to Canada [from the United States] to see how it would be here for single women ... [but] no matter how hard I try to please, I find myself under suspicion as people wonder why a fairly educated person who understands music should be here alone. No matter how many times over they are told the truth, and even see letters and papers that should show for themselves. I never go out evenings, and only go where this business [of teaching] leads, and they know all about every move, yet they do not seem to be able to understand and I wonder why, and try to be patient. I do not think it is a good country for single women under such conditions. They seem to think it strange I did not come to get married, and, according to my belief, I cannot get married until I meet the right one, and as I am a middle-aged woman, widow, and 'not handsome,' the chance of meeting the right one is not very good....

Idea [schoolteacher]

September 1910
Perdue, Saskatchewan

Sir,
... Most of the readers seem to be interested in matrimony. Well, I suppose I might be, too, if I happened to meet Mr. Right, but I find the subject of "Equal Rights" for women a good way to put all matrimonial notions out of one's head. I earn between seven and eight hundred a year, and have lots of spare time, too. Now, wouldn't it be foolish to bind myself even as a willing slave for the rest of my days? Just think of never having a "five" of your own, even though your working hours be from daylight till dark. How would you like it bachelors? Do write and tell us.

Bashful Bess

November 1910
Bladworth, Saskatchewan

Sir,
... Dear "Skittles," you have never been in love, that is evident, though possibly you have been disappointed in love; but allow me to say that if there was no love in this world the latter would stop.... Get married and you will learn very shortly that there is such a thing as love. But do not marry a man who does not love you.... I would never marry a girl 'till I had seen her and knew her, as, no matter what "Skittles" and others of like sentiment (or want of it) may say, without love life is not worth living. I know it, for I have lived without it too long, and one cannot fall in love with a photo. I would sooner do the cooking myself than marry just for a "cook"....

Contented as a Bach

November 1910
Longworth, Saskatchewan

Sir,

... I think that "Archibald" is very foolish. He must think that a woman was made for a slave. I think that a woman ought to have her own spending money as well as a man. She works hard all day, and in lots of cases harder than some men do. I do not think it is a woman's place to feed the hogs or milk the cows and do such work all the time.... I am afraid that one dress a year for the kitchen would not last very long if she had all the chores to do. Let me say, Mr. "Archibald," if you get a woman of the kind who will suit you, why, all right, but I think the girl who married you would be better off without you, for when single, she can go and do what she likes and handle her own purse.

A Rose Bud

November 1910

Sir,

... "Archibald"'s letter in the April number is really unique. On his account it is unfortunate that slavery has been abolished, otherwise he might spend a few dollars and supply himself with a household drudge. He will scarcely find in this twentieth century any damsel waiting at the well ready to let down and draw water for his camels. Ye gods and little fishes! but wouldn't that man's gall jar you? Wonder how far down the lane she, his prospective wife, would be expected to meet him with a smile and a steaming hot supper?... Oh Lord! Oh Lord! Where was he born and brought up, anyway? Poor Archibald!! I feel sorry that a man of such calibre has a foothold on Canadian soil. Let us hope his soul may grow and his heart—or is it only a gizzard—may expand and hollow somewhat before any woman ... puts herself in the power of such as he....

Atina [older woman]

January 1911
Calgary, Alberta

Sir,

... I have been ... not a little incensed at the attitude displayed by some of my sex who would assign to their wives the part of "a household drudge." With the last-mentioned class I have no sympathy whatever and certainly think they should remain bachelors until their ideals are changed. To my mind a woman should be a man's companion and stay, but that should not entail upon her the labour of doing outside work. In fact, she should be given aid in the many tasks which confront her in and around the home. Could more of our young men perceive the tact, patience and endurance which is required on the part of a woman to manage a home, I think their views on this point would be broadened and much of the unnecessary friction which occurs in the home life would be avoided. Hence, I say, let us endeavour to lighten the tasks of the women....

Acadian

February 1911
Mellowdale, Alberta

Sir,
... Now I think "Fiddlesticks" will admit that women have the greater responsibilities in the bringing up and training of children, and that the liquor traffic is one of the greatest curses they have to combat in the training of their children, boys especially. Now, it is my humble opinion that the granting of woman suffrage would be one of the greatest swats the liquor traffic ever received in this country, as I believe the women's votes would be the means of closing a good many hotels and bar-rooms.... And again, he says women are intended to be helpmates. Certainly they are; but by his letter he infers that the suffrage would hinder them from being our helpmates, while it would work just the very opposite; it would enable them to play the part of helpmate where they are now debarred, in cleaning up our country. I fail to see where the granting of woman suffrage would harmfully affect the home and home life, but, on the contrary, I think it would give the home and home life a great uplift....

Sod-Buster [male]

March 1911
Rocanville

Sir,
..."Archibald"'s letter ... expresses my sentiments exactly. Women of the present day are always howling about the amount of work they have to do, and if they get a chance to get together their sole conversation seems to be denouncing their neighbours or of fashions and how to get rid of the money that their husbands slave hard to gather. If there were some like the pioneer women of Ontario, who had to spin the yarn and weave the cloth and make all the clothes that the family wore, besides carrying the butter and eggs several miles to market, and when harvest time came get out in the field and bind sheaves by hand, and then do

the work that the present day woman finds such a drudge by way of a rest between meals. Those were women who could stand by a man and help him with the battles of life. I am a bachelor; my age is somewhere between thirty and fifty, and am not worrying much about matrimony, as I believe that it is easier to do my own housework than have a poor, weak "imitation of woman" killing herself with such strenuous an occupation as keeping house for a farmer—I am yours,

Admirer of Archibald

July 1911
Plateau, Saskatchewan

Sir,

… I am a married woman and have as good [a] husband as the average man makes…. Now, just a word to married men, especially. Treat your wife to a little "taffy stick" [love talk] once in a while. She may be snappy, if she hasn't been used to "taffy," but she doesn't mean to be. She is only so surprised and taken unawares that, womanlike, she must say something, and like as not, the second nice speech to her will find her ten or twenty years back to your old honeymoon days; and Mr. Man don't forget that your wife married you, as a love, and be a lover still, or you are obtaining a helpmate under false pretences. Then, see that she has clothes to look nice in … (your housekeeper would have them, if you had to hire one, and it's your money that would pay for them). Will you not treat your wife better than any hired help? And I am sure she will be happy. I am certain you will be and home will be a real home, not one in name only.

Winunla

July 1912
Dunallen, Manitoba

Dear Editor,

… I don't think a woman should be expected to do a great deal of chores [outside work]. I think that is the man's work, and a man should not be expected to scrub floors, wash dishes, and peel potatoes; that is a woman's work. But if a couple sincerely love each other they will not object to helping each other, and life will be much pleasanter….

Kitchenjammer [male]

November 1912
Tugaske, Saskatchewan

Dear Editor,
… Just a few words on the married woman subject. How many married women are there that get out as much as they should? But very few. Some man will say he has an old cranky woman. Why is she cranky? Because she never gets anywhere. I wonder how some of the men would like to be shut up in the house for a life-time; they would soon kick. And other men will go and throw their money over the bar and when the wife says there is something needed in the house why he will say: "You don't need that or you can get along without." Say, girls, I have a half section and am very lonely.…

The Barefoot Boy

January 1913
Saskatchewan

Dear Editor,
… I have heard a great deal and read more about the unhappiness of the marriages in the West, but judging from what I have observed since settling here I think that would be very strange were it otherwise when one considers how little real love there is in most of the marriages contracted here.… Is it reasonable to suppose, I say, that these bachelors really love or that marriage based on such principles can be happy for both? True, many of these married housekeepers are contented. But is contentment enough? Contentment is passive, happiness is active and marriage, if it is the result of a mutual love, not affection and esteem, will bring happiness, not merely contentment. It is time, I think, that some of the many who amuse themselves at the expense of those enterprising bachelors spoke a word of warning for the benefit of such unmarried women as may venture into this land of women hunters. I am not warning the girls against our Western bachelors. They are, as a rule, steady, sober men, a little gloomy maybe—their lonely lives tend to that. But I do warn them against a loveless marriage. Those men do not mean to practice deceit but they need companions and housekeepers, and can easily settle it with their conscience if they venture beyond the truth in their vows of undying devotion.… My belief is that a wife should be her husband's chief pride.… As it is, the average wife seems to be regarded as a necessary evil, and my firm belief is that these loveless marriages are going to be the curse of this otherwise glorious country.

Plato

February 1913
Duff, Saskatchewan

Dear Editor,
… I think it is selfish of a fellow to win the love and esteem of a girl, and then ask her to try and be contented in a little lumber shack about fourteen by sixteen feet, and into the same place she must combine parlour, dining-room and kitchen, and try and make herself think that she is really happy and contented. Would it not be just as well if the struggling sweetheart were to wait another year or two until he got a little better fixed?… I earnestly believe if you find the right one that she would be quite willing to wait a little longer while you made a happy little home.… In my travels up and down the country I have seen so many young women who have undertaken to brave the hardships of the first year or two on the farm with their husbands, only to find that when they are quite comfortable they have got out of the social circle and are contented to stay at home hard working as ever, with their freshness and pretty ways all gone, and such a sight should, I think, make us all careful.… I myself am content to wait until I can give my future wife a little comfort and some of the worldly goods, for I am a great believer in that old saying, "When poverty comes in at the door, love flies out of the window."

The Crank

March 1913
Saskatchewan

Dear Editor,
… "Is the uniting or legal union of man and woman for life a failure?"… In face of the frequently expressed masculine belief that all girls are ready to humbly pick up the handkerchief, when any "lord of creation" deigns to throw it, the fact remains that every day the average girl is less and less inclined to regard marriage as the end and aim of her existence. But, nevertheless, at an alarmingly early age, the busy working girl demands, "What has marriage to offer me?" Single, she works hard—true; but in her leisure moments she is absolutely free. She owes no man anything, and because she is happy, and healthy, and bright, all the men are pleased to be in her society, and help to give her a good time. She can be friends, "good comrades" with any or all of them. What would she gain in exchange? She looks in pitying fashion at the girls of her own age who have married, and are living, in her eyes, such narrow and uninteresting lives—slaves of the ring.… And is she wise? A busy, bustling, or more or less butterfly life may content her for a year or

two; but the day inevitably dawns when a woman's heart demands something more, when the sight of even the poorest of her sisters surrounded by husband and children, fills her soul with envy, and the isolation of her chosen lot frightens her. Then she longs for a home, not a mere shelter, but the dearest spot on earth, because it contains those she loves, and to whose happiness she is absolutely necessary. Don't refuse a good fellow who has half won your heart for no better reason than that you imagine you will have a better time as a girl bachelor. If husband and wife were to live as designed, in accordance as they vowed, it would be impossible to prove that marriage was other than "the grandest sphere of life"....

Brightside [male]

April 1913
Eastbrook, Saskatchewan

Dear Editor,
... Although I am no pen artist I will in my feeble way try to write a few lines in defence of we bachelors, who he ["Plato"] has so ably pictured as unloving woman hunters, whose sole ambition in life seems to be to enslave through faithless promises and marriage some unsuspecting and unsophisticated but loving girls, into being his unpaid housekeeper for the rest of his or her allotted time span.... Have roamed over a great part of this western country of ours, where I have seen and learned to know quite a few bachelors and their habits. Have found a large part of them to be young men with clean habits, a good education, refined manners and with a reverence for womankind that is to be found only in this country in the early years of homestead life.... Where can a man better learn to appreciate women than out in a lonely homestead shack, where with only the image of his mother and sisters to fill his mind, he learns through hard experience that the household tasks ... that women with a tenth of our strength, cheerfully do, are more tiring and tedious than their monotonous routine.... Who has a better chance to become the model husband, than the lonely bachelor, who has been through life's hard fire and come out well tempered with a knowledge of work not equally divided?...

Hank on the Homestead

May 1913
Saskatchewan

Dear Editor,
… It is true that there are many marriages, and married men and women of today, who marry for nothing but the business part of it. The man looks at it from his standpoint of view. He is tired of batching and living alone, and looks for a wife, and often the one he marries is one who is willing to take the first chance that comes along, and sell her life to the man merely for a home. It would be far better for a woman like this to go through life single than to live a life full of drudgery, and not enjoying herself in any way. But then there is the other side of marriage to look at, where people marry who love each other, and are both willing to sacrifice anything for each other's sake. They will live a happy life, and those are the people who go to prove that marriage is in the greater part a success.…

A Western Guy

May 1913
Alberta

Dear Editor,
… I would like to take up the affirmative side of the debate, viz., "Is Marriage a Failure," introduced by "Brightside" in the March issue.… Right here may I say, a contract such as marriage usually formed after an acquaintance of, say, two years, must invariably lead to disappointment or discontent later.… But let us look at the mutually happy couple. These form probably the largest percentages [of married couples].… Do they draw any material benefit? Maybe they do, but does not the world lose by it? These two people who are contented in their own companionship, are they not liable to forget their friends in need, their duty to others, charities, etc.? Also does not this same sense of contentment lead to the abandonment of aims that would have benefited others?… In all the civilized countries we find that women are gradually filling men's places; this tends to increase freedom of action and thought. They are no longer forced to look to men for their means of living in their mature years. While this is undoubtedly a blessing in many ways,… is it not apt to lead to loveless marriages, and consequently failures, by the crowding out of sentiment by commercialism? … I would advise all young people to seriously consider the matter [of marriage] before taking the final plunge, unless you have a few thousand to buy a divorce with.

A Confirmed Bachelor

June 1913
Saskatchewan

Dear Editor,
... There has been a question asked a few times whether young people should get married, or should they wait till the man has made his money first.... I don't think there is anything made by waiting. I have tried that myself, and I have taken good notice of the fair sex as I went along. I am better off now than when I started out, but haven't found anything better in the line of women. A fine little lady who is willing to brave the storm with you is worth half a dozen of them that want to wait for your money so she won't have anything to do but spend it....

Teetotaller

August 1913
Manitoba

Dear Editor,
... [Regarding] the publication of a letter in your May issue over the pen name of "A Confirmed Bachelor." His letter made me sit up and take notice, for it is the most disgraceful bit of sophistry that I have read for many a day. It would be interesting to know just what causes a man's mind to become so morbid as to render him capable of condemning the sacred bonds of matrimony. Marriage ... is the moral foundation of society ... and upon its success or failure depends our whole social system.... Surely our correspondent doesn't think this nation is on the downward road to destruction—or on the verge of disparity and immorality! No, marriage is not a failure by any means. It is only those who should not marry, and do, that makes a failure of it.... Marriage is never a failure when founded on love, toleration and common sense....

Dumpy [male]

October 1913
Saskatchewan

Dear Editor,
... A picture which no artist can do justice to is to see a little home where husband and wife are all in all to each other, each trying their utmost to make a little heaven of their home. This is where we find true love reigns supreme, and ... it is among those who do not make the almighty dollar their god that true love and happiness is mostly to be found. Marriage where love reigns supreme, even though the home be humble, is far ahead of the splendour of the mansion where the

marriage was made for riches. Money will do most things, but it cannot purchase love and happiness....

Qui Vive [male]

April 1914
Manitoba

Dear Editor,
… There seems to be a lot of discussion in these pages as to whether or not "Marriage is a Failure".…I don't for a moment think it is, but there are so many couples married who are not suited to one another in any respect, and it is surely a failure as far as they are concerned. So I think it behooves people to look before they leap, and be very very sure their love is a lasting one, and not a mere passion that will pass away when the novelty wears off, for it surely takes all the love there is to tide over the rough places....

Sammy [female]

May 1914
Moosomin, Saskatchewan

Dear Editor,
… Well, there are quite a few questions now on woman suffrage being discussed. As for my part, I don't care much which way it goes, for I think if a woman stays at home and keeps her house clean and tidy, always has a nice hot meal cooked for her good man and meets him with a smile, and does as she ought to she will be treated kindly without running all over to every meeting that she can hear tell of within twenty-five miles of her. Come now, all you members, let us know what you think of it....

Honey Dew [female]

December 1914
British Columbia

Dear Editor,
… Women's votes are needed here just as much as they are in the Old Country. A woman works for her family, indoors, and as a drudge and gets very poor pay too. Why shouldn't she get a vote just as much as some drunken old sot of a man who has wasted his brains at the bar? Why shouldn't women get a vote? She has to live under the laws after they are made, so why shouldn't she get a chance to say how they are to be made? … If a woman had a vote saloons would be few and far between. Women have to stand a drunken husband coming

home and abusing them, and yet he gives the vote that keeps that awful curse in power....

One Girl in B.C.

February 1915
Scandia, Saskatchewan

Dear Editor,
... I suppose all married couples are so well pleased and their time is so well taken up that they have no time for corresponding, but I, for my part, would like to see a letter in the *W.H.M.* from them. We bachelors would like to hear from those that have hitched up in double harness, and find out how they like it. We, Us and Co., have kind of figured on accepting a partner when the chance comes, so a few instructions from those who have gone through the mill would be appreciated. Here is something to discuss: "Which is happier: a married or a single man?" I will sign myself,

The Village Blacksmith

April 1915

Dear Friends,
... One thing that strikes an Easterner like myself (have only been transplanted a few years and can't as yet wax enthusiastic over the treeless prairies), is the way the Western bachelor can cook.... I should imagine they would make ideal husbands, because they would know just what a woman is tied down to after she is married. You know the Eastern men think all there is to housework is meals. Bless us, wouldn't a woman get off easy if all she had to do was cook three meals?...

Freda

May 1915
Kerrobert, Saskatchewan

Dear Editor,
... There is much diversity of opinion on this subject [of love].... Truly, love is worth seeking, is worth keeping when found, is worth hardship, privation and many other sacrifices, save honour, for love without honour is nil. Love is the greatest blessing in this world; it is the Divine spark straight from God. Without it the world would be cold indeed. Hold it not lightly my fellow-readers. Be assured that it will repay you ten thousand-fold for any sacrifice you make in its cause. I would rather be poor as I am, with the wealth of love I possess of husband and friends, than rich in this world's goods minus love....

Contented

July 1915
Landis, Saskatchewan

Dear Editor,
... I see by the "Village Blacksmith" that he would like to hear from a married man. As I am one, perhaps I can answer him.... Well, I think that double harness is all right, provided the collar and hames fit, but if not, it's a poor business. As for my wife and I, it is all right. I would not want to discourage any couple from getting married as it is the best business that can happen, especially for a farmer, who after working all day in the field, can come in and sit down to a decent meal.... A "bach" has no time to cook while working and doesn't feel like doing so when he isn't. The "Village Blacksmith" also says "Which is the happier, married or single?" Well, I say that if a wife does get cranky once in a while, we men have more fun and can beat it for the barn if need be, and if she doesn't get angry occasionally, she is a poor stick....

A Reformed Bach

November 1915

Dear Editor,
... I have been raised on a farm and have always liked it. If I ever married I should want to make my home on one. Of course I am not seriously thinking of matrimonial matters, being only eighteen. I think I have lots of time to consider that very important question. So many marry too young and then repent the remainder of their days. It is quite alright for one to marry young if they can see their way clear and know the man.... Some girls think they know their husbands until they get them, and then they find that they didn't know them at all (only their better qualities)....

Valley Flower [female]

May 1918

Dear Editor,
... There is a subject I should like to hear discussed in your columns: "Does love grow less after marriage?" From what I have seen it seems that a couple before marriage can be madly in love with each other but after about five years of married life they very seldom even kiss one another. Is it true that marriage kills love? Now let us hear from some of those who have experience on this subject as I being single can only speak of what I have seen....

A Western Bach

July 1918

Dear Editor,
... "A Western Bach" brings up an interesting subject for discussion, namely, "Does love grow less after marriage." I don't think it does. He says that it seems that a couple before marriage can be madly in love with each other, but after about five years they very seldom even kiss one another. This may be true, but great men say that human beings are never satisfied. They long for and strive after one particular object and when they get it they want something else. So I suppose that before marriage they want each other desperately.... Then after they are married they wonder what all the rush was about.... Of course, there are exceptions where one may find couples who love each other "till death do them part" and then some, and I sincerely hope in this case the exceptions are greater than the rule. Sincerely yours,

Irish Nora

October 1918

Dear Editor,
... Yes, "Western Bach," love does in a great many cases grow less after marriage, but let me say that in almost every case, the fault lies with the husband.... "Western Bach," if you are contemplating marriage and want the happiness of your honeymoon to last, make that honeymoon extend to where the parting [death] comes. How many of our western women are heart hungry for some of the love, the endearing words and fond embraces of the first year of their married life? Husband has more land, more stock, more machinery, more work. He works so hard he is often irritable and cross. His thoughts and attentions are entirely taken up with his work. The little woman whom he promised to love and cherish plods along doing her best and being always faithful. He has forgotten the time when he used to take her in his arms and kiss her.... In the rush and worry, the difficulties and problems of this western life, a few minutes thus spent with wifie will mean so much to him and a thousand times more to her. And love will not grow less but will ever grow and bloom and blossom in happiness in their home, and in their lives.

Lonely [male]

November 1918

Dear Editor,
... I see in your paper where the question arises, "Does Marriage Kill Love?" Well, I think where the young folks get too strong-headed

This rather unusual wedding took place in the 1920s in Redcliffe, AB. Medicine Hat Archives / PC263.1

and selfish, it always happens so. One thinks himself better than the other and love flies out of the window, leaving one moping in the corner, while the other goes his own way to seek a little comfort. I have seen women who even forget their husbands "over there." They would become vain and selfish, and then the law would step in and take away their little ones, because they proved to be traitors to their husbands. A pretty face and form is a lure, and when a woman knows this she should safeguard against it and stand firm beyond all, as the boys do against the Huns. I have learned many a lesson since I have been left alone. My strong mind keeps me in safety, because where one [the flesh] is weak the other should be firm and steady. It takes a woman to ruin a man, and it also takes a woman to make a man. "The hand that rocks the cradle" should always be steady and true in all things....

A Soldier's Wife

December 1919

Dear Editor and Readers,
... Very often we hear it asked why so many married women, with comfortable homes, and husbands who are able to provide for them, go out to work, or try to earn money of their very own at home.... If the husband, according to his salary, wages or income from whatever source, would every week allow the wife a little change for her personal use, she would be all the happier—and so would he. I am not alluding to the extravagant woman who always drags a man down, but to the economical, hardworking, patient, loving, faithful one, who makes home a paradise for the man who appreciates her—and who is in the large majority. If he would get a little bank or box, and drop in what he could afford or as much as his generosity permitted him to ... and say, "There, dear, is a little pin-money for you; do what you like with it," why, in no time she would have quite an accumulation. And think how much happier she would be, knowing she had it there to use for any trifle she might wish for; all women love pretty things, you know.... Bless the dear, true little wife; she deserves a generous allowance, for she rightfully earns it.... Just think this over, husbands. Some women ... go out to work to help meet the family expenses,... but, as a rule, I think it is the desire for independence that takes married women from the homes, and a proper "sharing" of the income would do away with this.

Fair Play [female]

Notes

Notes to Introduction, pgs 1–5

1. The *WHM* was founded in Winnipeg in 1899. In 1905 its circulation was twenty thousand. In the two or three years before it became a national magazine in 1932 (known as the *National Home Monthly*), its circulation grew to 103,000, the second highest in Canada. *Western Home Monthly*, March 1905, p. 10; F. Sutherland, *The Monthly Epic: A History of Canadian Magazines* (Markham, Ont.: Fitzhenry and Whiteside, 1989), p. 160.

2. One indication of the column's popularity was the editor's note in the June 1909 issue that the magazine was able to print only "one letter out of every twenty that comes to us"—it was publishing nearly thirty letters each month—and his urgent plea for "our correspondents to be as brief as possible." *WHM*, June 1909, p. 18.

3. Often these efforts bore fruit. "Through your valuable assistance," wrote an appreciative Alberta man, "I have already got several lady correspondents with a view to matrimony. Your help is much needed indeed sir by many of us lonely bachelors who have not the necessary time to leave our homes and stock on a wife hunting expedition." *WHM*, April 1906, p. 14 ("Alberta boy"). As well, the *WHM* reported in the September and November issues of 1907 that at least four couples had married that year as a result of the Correspondence column.

4. As the population—especially the female population—of western Canada increased, and as passenger-train service became more widely available, it was easier for single men and women to meet in person. By 1921 fifty-five percent of the rural male population on the Prairies was married, which was close to the national average. Hence the need for a matrimonial column declined over time. G. Friesen, *The Canadian Prairies: A History* (Toronto: University of Toronto Press, 1987), p. 166.

5. This figure is based on 227 months' worth of columns, each containing an average of 14.5 letters. The *WHM* seems to have been published every month without fail for the entire run of the column, and between November 1905 and October 1924 the column appeared in every issue except one.

6. Given the geographic origin of the letters in the Correspondence column between 1905 and mid-1916, during which such information was included, the letters may not seem to represent Canadian opinion generally: 36 percent were sent from Saskatchewan, 23 percent from Manitoba, 21 percent from Alberta, 7 percent from Ontario, 5 percent from British Columbia, 2 percent from the Maritime provinces and Newfoundland, 1 percent from Quebec, and 5 percent from outside the country. In short, 80 percent of the letters came from the three prairie provinces. But of the roughly nine hundred thousand people who came to the Prairies between 1896 and 1914 (when the region's population at the start of the period was approximately three hundred thousand), just under one-third came from central and eastern Canada; even many American immigrants were returning Canadians. On the surface, then, the regional nature of the letters is overstated. So is the class/occupational dimension, since most British immigrants who came to the Prairies were previously of working-class background, and 75 percent of prairie farmers supplemented their income with part-time wage labour on the railroads, in the mines, and in logging camps. It is worth noting, as well, that by 1911, 35 percent of prairie residents lived in urban areas. Friesen, *The Canadian Prairies,* pp. 319, 512, 514; D. Kerr and D. Holdsworth, eds.,

Historical Atlas of Canada: Addressing the Twentieth Century, vol. III, plate 27; R. Cook and R. Brown, *Canada 1896–1921: A Nation Transformed*, pp. 54–62.

7. At the time, a "bachelor" was defined as a man who lived on his own or with other men and was usually single (married men who worked the land in advance of their wives' arrival were also considered bachelors). However, if he lived at home or with another family—if there was a female in the household—he was not considered a bachelor. C. Danysk, "'A Bachelor's Paradise': Homesteaders, Hired Hands, and the Construction of Masculinity, 1880–1930," in C. Cavanaugh and J. Mouat, eds., *Making Western Canada: Essays on European Colonization and Settlement*, pp. 154–85.

8. E. Silverman, "Women's Perceptions of Marriage on the Alberta Frontier," in D. Jones and I. MacPherson, eds., *Building Beyond the Homestead* (Calgary: University of Calgary Press, 1988), pp. 54–55.

9. Kerr and Holdsworth, *Historical Atlas of Canada*, plate 27.

10. February 1916, p. 53 ("A City Girl").

11. See April 1916, pp. 60–61.

Notes to Chapter 1, pgs 7–20

1. *WHM*, August 1907, p. 15. Excerpt from a poem written by a farmer from Bunker Hill, Manitoba.

2. In 1901 most of southern Manitoba and southeastern Saskatchewan (then part of the Northwest Territories) had a density of at least two persons per square mile. Much of central and western Saskatchewan and eastern Alberta did not reach this density until the second decade of the twentieth century. Kerr and Holdsworth, eds., *Historical Atlas*, plate 17.

3. The ratio of adult men (over twenty-one) to adult women on the prairies in 1911 was 138:100 in Manitoba, 181:100 in Saskatchewan, and 184:100 in Alberta. Danysk, "'A Bachelor's Paradise,'" p. 181n.

4. Several male correspondents supported the right of all women (instead of only widowed, deserted, or divorced women) to be granted homesteads on the grounds that it would alleviate the loneliness of bachelor homesteaders. See, for example, the letters from "Engineer," August 1914, p. 63, and "Thirty-Two," February 1914, p. 62.

5. December 1911, p. 10 ("Coulee Bill").

6. November 1905, p. 44 ("Marriageable Widow").

7. P. Ward, *Courtship, Love, and Marriage in Nineteenth-Century English Canada* (Montreal and Kingston: McGill-Queen's University Press, 1990), chap. 4. Ward notes that the restrictions on the movements of city women began to ease after 1880, indicating that some change was occurring. While we still know too little about courtship etiquette in the early twentieth century, the letters in the *Western Home Monthly's* Correspondence column on this issue (see chap. 4) indicate that Canadian society still expected men to take the initiative in matters of romance.

8. November 1906, p. 8.

9. May 1914, p. 77 ("Honey Dew").

Notes to Chapter 2, pgs 21–44

1. March 1906, p. 38.

2. January 1907, p. 14 ("Woman's Friend").

3. May 1906, p. 6 ("Not Particular").

4. For a lively portrait of the "booze and brothel" syndrome in western Canada in these years, see J. Gray's *Red Lights on the Prairies* (Toronto: Macmillan, 1971) and B. Broadfoot, *The Pioneer Years 1895–1914* (Toronto: Doubleday Canada Ltd., 1976), pp. 254–57, 313. It is no wonder that prohibitionist sentiment was strongest in the West,

particularly among women, and that Prohibition was first implemented here provincially during World War One.

5. February 1907, p. 10 ("Danger").
6. May 1908, p. 20 ("Quick March").
7. October 1907, p. 15 ("Busybody").
8. A good overview of this phenomenon may be found in R. Cook, *The Regenerators: Social Criticism in Late Victorian English Canada* (Toronto: University of Toronto Press, 1985), chap. 2.
9. S. F. Wise, "Sport and Class Values in Old Ontario and Quebec," in M. Mott, ed., *Sports in Canada: Historical Readings* (Toronto: Copp Clark Pitman Ltd., 1989), pp.107–29; A. Metcalfe, *Canada Learns to Play: The Emergence of Organized Sport, 1807–1914* (Toronto: McClelland and Stewart, 1987), chap. 3.
10. January 1913, p. 87 ("Diamond Dick, Jr.").
11. By this point in the column's evolution, it is not clear whether the writers' intentions were romantic. Unless correspondents specifically requested letters from the opposite sex or mentioned their "ideal" man or woman, I neither considered their comments for my analysis, nor included their letters in the book.
12. August 1907, p. 18 ("Canadian Jack").
13. November 1908, p. 16.

Notes to Chapter 3, pgs 45-80

1. May 1906, p. 18 ("Disgusted").
2. February 1907, p. 13 ("Bob of Saskatoon").
3. While men rarely specified good character or morals as prerequisites in prospective female partners, several expressed their intolerance for "intemperate" women who either drank, smoked, danced, swore, played cards, or engaged in other "immoral" activities. See, for example, "BC Optimist," January 1909, p. 12, and "Honky Domm," May 1909, p. 21.
4. A. Prentice, et. al., *Canadian Women: A History*, 2nd ed. (Toronto: Harcourt Brace Canada, 1996), pp. 155–62, 189–94.
5. Given that many young English women who came to western Canada in these years were from the educated urban middle class, and hence relatively deficient in both farming and even domestic skills, this belief appears to have been justified. S. Sundberg, "Farm Women on the Canadian Prairie Frontier: The Helpmate Image," in V. Strong-Boag and A. Fellman, eds., *Rethinking Canada: The Promise of Women's History*, pp. 95–106. It's worth noting, too, that the reputation of *male* English immigrants who tried their hand at farming wasn't much better. See Broadfoot, *The Pioneer Years 1895–1914*, pp. 136–43, 210–11.
6. February 1907, p. 12 ("Romola").
7. September 1907, p. 14 ("Cheerful Canadian").
8. July 1911, p. 82.
9. October 1910, p. 78 ("Red, White, and Blue"). Emphasis added.
10. July 1912, p. 92.
11. On the whole the war did not change the definition of the ideal woman in the way it did the definition of the ideal man. Male correspondents sometimes expressed admiration for the patriotic efforts of women, but they rarely made these efforts a prerequisite to a romantic relationship in the way that women did with prospective male partners.
12. August 1907, p. 16 ("Boston Boy").
13. It is not always clear in the postwar letters whether the intentions of the correspondents were romantic. Unless they requested letters from the opposite sex or specifically described the "ideal" woman, I did not include such letters in my analysis or in

the letters in this chapter.
14. May 1920, p. 62 ("Violin Lover").
15. December 1909, p. 34 ("The Little Dark Girl").

Notes to Chapter 4, pgs 81-108

1. September 1907, p. 16.
2. See P. Ward, "Courtship and Social Space in Nineteenth-Century English Canada," *Canadian Historical Review* 68:1 (March 1987), pp. 35–62.
3. For example, one man wrote that "I don't want to be put on the matrimonial list as yet, but would just like to get acquainted with some of the fairer sex, which might possibly lead to the all-important question." May 1911, p. 87 ("Semper Fidelis").
4. January 1908, p. 14 ("White Pine").
5. December 1906, p. 68 ("William Wary").
6. January 1910, p. 19 ("St. Nick").
7. January 1907, p. 15 ("Ellen").
8. No doubt the preponderance of men over women in the West, where most of the *WHM's* subscribers resided, partly explains this disparity.
9. One example comes from a 1912 letter from a woman calling herself "Girlie." "Yes, … leap year is certainly here," she wrote, "and a good thing for some of us that it is. So be careful, some of you 'handsome' boys, or first thing you know some 'old maid' will be proposing to you." March 1912, p. 84.
10. October 1913, p. 68 ("Cap").
11. Two examples of this phenomenon are the letter from "Bashful Kid," October 1918, p. 46, and from "Golden West," January 1909, p. 15.
12. August 1907, p. 18 ("Another Scotch Lassie").
13. November 1906, p. 8 ("White Head").
14. December 1909, p. 34 ("A Colchester Boy").

Notes to Chapter 5, pgs 109–126

1. Surveys of attitudes toward sexuality in Canada are woefully lacking for this period. The best is probably J. Cassels, *The Secret Plague: Venereal Disease in Canada, 1838–1939* (Toronto: University of Toronto Press, 1987), chap. 4.; M. Bliss, "'Pure Books on Avoided Subjects': Pre-Freudian Sexual Ideas in Canada," in *Historical Papers*, 1970, pp. 89–108, is also useful. For information on the intensified efforts of the Protestant middle class ("social purity" crusaders) to protect the morality of young working women, see C. Strange, *Toronto's Girl Problem: The Perils and Pleasures of the City, 1880–1930* (Toronto: University of Toronto Press, 1995), especially chap. 5.
2. The little research that exists on the issue of sexuality indicates this to be true. Women, in particular, were expected to exercise sexual self-restraint, during marriage and especially prior to it. Research on American attitudes is better. It, too, shows a high degree of prudishness within the urban Protestant middle class, with more liberal attitudes among the urban working class and some ethnic minorities, particularly with respect to premarital sex. Prentice, *Canadian Women*, pp. 166–67; Cassels, *The Secret Plague*, chap. 4; Strange, *Toronto's Girl Problem*, especially chaps. 3 and 5; John D'Emilio and Estelle Freedman, *Intimate Matters: A History of Sexuality in America* (New York: Harper and Row, 1988), pp. 176–77, 184–85.
3. January 1907, p. 12 ("Looking for a Partner").
4. September 1908, p. 14 ("Arrah Wanna").
5. See July 1910, pp. 94–95 ("Wild Rose"), and June 1911, p. 84 ("Lily of the Valley").
6. February 1907, p. 13 ("Patrick"). A writer calling himself "Sportsman" made the same stipulation in the October 1906 issue (p. 11).

7. June 1907, p. 16 ("Wakopa Boy").

8. A number of letters refer to couples "making love" or being "lovers," but at the time these terms meant mostly verbal expressions of love and, occasionally, some form of mild physical affection such as caressing; they certainly did not mean sexual intercourse.

9. One suspects that had the number of working-class individuals writing to the *Western Home Monthly* been higher, the picture of prewar prudishness might have been somewhat different. (See n. 2.)

10. Gray, *Red Lights* (see chap. 2, n. 4). A similar gender gap existed in the United States, within the urban Protestant middle class and certain ethnic groups. See D'Emilio and Freedman, *Intimate Matters*, chap. 8.

Notes to Chapter 6, pgs 127–161

1. It is worth noting that for some reason the issue of marriage was addressed almost exclusively by westerners. The views in this section are therefore less representative of cross-Canada opinion than those in the other chapters.

2. May 1908, p. 22 ("A Juggler"). Single working women, such as teachers, were also viewed with suspicion by the community. According to one historian, they were thought to be living unconventional, perhaps even immoral lives. Silverman, "Women's Perceptions of Marriage on the Alberta Frontier," p. 54 (see introduction, n. 8).

3. June 1906, p. 11 ("Jennie B.").

4. February 1906, p. 49 ("A Lover of Home Life").

5. What's more, adultery was the minimum grounds for divorce. When wives sought divorce, they also had to prove an additional hardship, such as extreme cruelty, incest, bigamy, or desertion. J. Snell, "'The White Life for Two': The Defence of Marriage and Sexual Morality in Canada, 1890–1914," in B. Bradbury, ed., *Canadian Family History: Selected Readings* (Toronto: Copp Clark Pitman Ltd., 1992), pp. 381–400; Prentice et. al., *Canadian Women*, p. 160 (see chap. 3, n. 4).

6. July 1907, p. 15 ("Trixie").

7. August 1907, p. 16 ("Busy Bee").

8. November 1906, p. 8 ("Lonely")

9. One Saskatchewan woman urged women not to marry if they already had a good home, "unless they love, then it is different. Girls, widows and spinsters, be careful whom you marry; it is for a lifetime, until 'death do us part.'" July 1906, p. 22 ("Susan").

10. This would also explain why many readers opposed short courtship periods, courtship by correspondence, and getting married too young, for all were seen to hinder the development of true love between men and women.

11. Unfortunately, the views of married people are mostly absent from the column. It would have been interesting to read their thoughts on what made marriages work based on firsthand experience.

12. December 1906, p. 68 ("William Wary").

13. March 1919, p. 42 ("Free Agent").

14. Snell, "'The White Life for Two,'" p. 382. The pessimism was clearly exaggerated, for the percentage of men and women (over age fifteen) who were married actually rose between 1910 and 1919, by 5 and 2 percent respectively. Prentice, *Canadian Women*, p. 468, Table A.2 (see chap. 3, n. 4).

15. June 1910, p. 76 ("Primrose").

16. September 1910, p. 82 ("Wild Mack").

17. April 1916, p. 61 ("Rocky").